WHAT TO EXPECT IN SEMINARY

WHAT TO EXPECT IN SEMINARY

*Theological Education
as Spiritual Formation*

VIRGINIA SAMUEL CETUK

Abingdon Press
Nashville

WHAT TO EXPECT IN SEMINARY

Copyright © 1998 by Abingdon Press

This book is printed on elemental-chlorine-free paper.

Library of Congress Cataloging-in-Publication Data

Cetuk, Virginia Samuel, 1951–
    What to expect in seminary : theological education as spiritual formation / Virginia Samuel Cetuk.
      p. cm.
    Includes bibliographical references and index.
    ISBN 0-687-01728-9 (pbk. : alk. paper)
    1. Theological seminaries. 2. Theology—Study and teaching.
    3. Seminarians—Religious life. 4. Spiritual formation. I. Title.
BV4020.C48   1998
230'.071'1—dc21   98-35777
                                                       CIP

06 07 08 09 10 11 12 13 14 15 — 20 19 18 17 16 15 14 13 12 11

MANUFACTURED IN THE UNITED STATES OF AMERICA

For Norm,
my beloved husband and friend

And our sons,
Russell and Mitchell,
who are my pride and joy

"But those who wait for the LORD
shall renew their strength,
they shall mount up with wings like eagles,
they shall run and not be weary,
they shall walk and not faint."
(Isaiah 40:31)

CONTENTS

ACKNOWLEDGMENTS

he writing of a book, I have learned, is a communal effort. Though I have been the one sitting at the computer, I have been surrounded by a great cloud of witnesses. They have helped me, challenged me, supported me, and in the words of Nelle Morton, they have "heard me into speech" through their comments, questions, and encouragement. I want to publicly thank them here.

The first person I spoke with about this project was Dr. Robin Lovin, now Dean of Perkins School of Theology. He was enthusiastic about the idea and put me in touch with Dr. Rex Matthews, formerly of Abingdon Press. Both men helped me develop the idea for the book further and guided me through the early stages of the process. I am grateful to them for their early belief in me and this book.

With Rex's departure, I gained a new editor. Having never written a book before, I was uncertain of her role relative to my writing. She has guided me through the process with grace and patience and good humor.

Along the way I have shared chapters with Dr. Janet Fishburn, now retired from the Drew Theological School faculty. Janet's insights about theological school students, theological education, and ministry are always on target, and I have learned much from her over the years that not only shaped me as a theological educator but helped me to write this book.

The Reverend Barbara Troxell was an early reader of portions of the manuscript. Currently the Director of Field Education at Garrett-Evangelical Seminary in Evanston, Illinois, Barbara has a profound spiritual life that she shares freely with students and colleagues. Her spirit matches the spirit of this book beautifully, and I am grateful for her support and encouragement.

Because I have written this while serving full time as Associate

Dean for Contextual Learning at Drew I have had to find ways to fit the writing around my ongoing responsibilities. Dean Leonard Sweet has been unfailingly supportive and encouraging of me throughout this long writing season. He allowed me to take a leave last year and encouraged me to take as much of the summer as I needed in order to complete the project. He has offered spiritual support as well. Being deeply committed to spiritual formation through theological education, he has served as a mentor as well as a friend, and I am deeply grateful to him.

Thanks also to my family for their encouragement. My sister, Linda Samuel Bickford, and brother, James Samuel, have consistently offered helpful comments that served to urge me on to completion of the task. Although neither one of them is in theological education, they are both spiritually mature and understand the discipline necessary to finish this book. I rejoice that they are my siblings and am grateful for their help in this project.

Although my mother, Merle Samuel, now suffers from Alzheimer's disease and no longer knows what I do in my work, she was aware that I was beginning to write this book a few years ago and was enormously proud of me then. I am grateful that I often told her that she was my earliest and most profound model of mature spirituality. Indeed, her spirit infuses my life and work and is evident on every page of the manuscript. How blessed I am to be her daughter.

Finally I would like to acknowledge my husband Norman, my partner in life for more than twenty-five years. Because he has worked in law enforcement for nearly the same amount of time, his perspective on much of life is different from mine, as you might imagine. Our conversations about important issues are often lively and interesting, and I have learned a lot from him about what it means to have the "common sense" he loves so well. His encouragement in the writing of this book has been the underlying foundation for the project—he knew I could do it before I did. It is to him and to our sons, Russell and Mitchell, that this book is dedicated.

Drew Theological School
Madison, New Jersey

INTRODUCTION

But those who wait for the LORD . . . *shall mount
up with wings like eagles.*   Isaiah 40:31

or nearly sixteen years at Drew Theological School I have worked closely with students who are preparing themselves to be in ministry of one kind or another. Because of my different roles—Director of Contextual Learning/ Supervised Ministry, Associate Dean, teacher, counselor, mentor—I have had many conversations with students about their experiences in seminary. With the passage of time I no longer always remember which student graduated in which year, where students serve in ministry, or even whether or not they were ordained after graduating. To be sure, the students who come to Drew are unique and defy categorizing. Our students are quite diverse with respect to age, background, ethnicity, denomination, family circumstance, and lifestyle, and to draw too many conclusions about the student body as a whole would be risky. There are some points, however, at which students seem remarkably similar, like their view of the rigors of seminary life and ministerial preparation.

For the past several years I have noticed a tendency on the part of some students to view the seminary experience in a somewhat negative light. Instead of expecting it to be demanding and challenging in every way, they sometimes seem to expect to graduate in three years without being seriously and personally challenged.

I am not saying that these students do not expect to have a lot of reading and writing to do or that they do not expect the reading to be challenging in some way. Rather, it is almost as if they are surprised when they are pushed to reexamine the faith commitments they bring with them to seminary and, in effect, led to ask themselves whether they do indeed have a mature faith and if they do not, what they will do about it.

Such naivete about the rigors of graduate school work surprises me. "How could you expect seminary, which is, after all, graduate work, to be anything but demanding and challenging on every level of your being?" I have often wanted to say. Their response is contrary to what is needed for a lively and optimistic ministry.

Confronted with my own mortality in a new way after a serious illness in 1991, I began to see this negativity on the part of students as the spirit of fear it really is and decided to write this book in response. The heart of this book is about the choice all seminarians have in the ways they meet the various challenges of theological education. As a seminarian, you can choose to see each area of the seminary experience as something that contributes to your spiritual formation and reliance upon God, or as something that is to be feared and defended against lest it lead you farther away from God.

In the chapters that follow, I suggest theological education can be a time of spiritual formation. In chapter 1 I review the tasks of ministry in general terms and invite you to think about yourself in relation to them. Chapter 2 introduces the theoretical concept of *reframing* as a lens through which to view your theological education.

In the third chapter I discuss the decision to enter seminary and the implications for your "former life." Students enter a program of theological education for many different reasons, looking for and hoping for different things, and are open to different experiences and kinds of learning. This chapter will explore the nature of the "call to ministry" and its implications for the way one views the seminary experience.

Chapter 4 explores the impact of being in a diverse community of people of different ages, backgrounds, theologies, vocational paths, ontological understandings, and styles of relating. We will also consider the physical, emotional, and spiritual dimensions of living in the community.

Chapter 5 examines the impact of critical thinking upon your faith commitments and spiritual life. What happens, for example, when students are introduced to form and literary criticism and learn to separate the sayings of Jesus from the sayings of the early church?

Chapter 6 will help you to think about the impact of your field education experience on your developing vocational identity and spiritual formation. We will look at the process of evaluation at the center of supervised ministry as an exercise in the discernment of God's will and direction for your life.

Chapter 7 raises issues of life in the material world. In particular we will look at the financial realities of enrolling in a program of theological education and consider issues of time management.

For your spiritual growth, and to help you think more clearly about the true nature of your opportunity, each chapter concludes with an exercise designed to assist you to address with God the issues raised in that chapter. The inclusion of these exercises reframes this study as devotional literature along with a guide to the journey of theological education in general.

In the book of Isaiah we read about the two kinds of people: those who wait upon God and those who do not. Isaiah's message is clear—even the young will fall and become weary if they do not rely upon God. Those who do walk closely with God and expect God's help will not be disappointed. They shall

> renew their strength, they shall mount up with wings like eagles, they shall run and not be weary, they shall walk and not faint. (Isaiah 40:31)

Chapter 1

The Tasks of Ministry

Woe to me if I do not proclaim the gospel! 1 Corinthians 9:16

hen I was seven years old the bishop sent our church a new pastor. Almost immediately I transferred my intense loyalty from the outgoing pastor to the new pastor. It was not that I did not love the former pastor anymore; it was simply that Rev. Adams was so loving and friendly that this seven-year-old quickly found a new and good friend. He was tall and thin, had already lost most of his gray hair, and wore glasses that only served to magnify the perpetual twinkle in his eye. While moving through his busy schedule each week, and in the midst of a large and growing congregation, he always seemed to find time for the children around him. When I was with him I felt as if I were the most important person in the world, and under his leadership my own faith life was nurtured and deepened.

One Sunday when I was eleven years old I attended church with my family as was our custom. I can still recall watching Rev. Adams move about the front of the church that day during the worship service. At one point he walked across the altar area from his chair to the communion table. While he was walking I said to myself, "If I could be just like Rev. Adams, I would be a minister." Although I immediately chided myself for having such an impossible dream, a new idea had taken root in my soul—I could be a minister!

Two years later I was reading a book by James Bishop called *The Day Christ Died* and suddenly felt a Presence in the room with me. In a twinkling I felt the Presence wash over me in an indescribably beautiful way. In those moments, so different from the moments just before and just after, I knew with a deep, deep certainty that I was loved and that God wanted me to be an ordained minister.

When I shared the news of my call to ministry with my parents, they were supportive and enthusiastic.[1] When I told Rev. Adams about my call and intention to pursue ordination, he was delighted! Rev. Adams and my father arranged for the bishop to meet me (not the other way around!) so that he could know one of his budding clergy. That the bishop counseled me to marry a minister instead of becoming one myself did nothing to dampen the enthusiasm and support of my pastor and my parents. (It did, however, dampen the enthusiasm and support my parents and pastor had for the bishop!)

As I look back across the years to that time in my life, I realize that Rev. Adams not only was a tremendous support to me as I matured in the faith, he remains to this day the first and the most influential model I had for ministry.

No doubt you also have models for ministry who have shaped your desire to enter seminary and pursue a life of service to others in the name of Jesus Christ. Our models come from the ranks of both clergy and laity to be sure. Some of our most precious and powerful memories of church are those we have of our Sunday school teachers, who helped us memorize Bible verses, gave us juice and cookies, and talked to us about what was important in our lives.

Who were the people who became your models for ministry? Perhaps it was your pastor who, like Rev. Adams, radiated a joy that seemed unending and showed how much fun it could be to serve others. Perhaps it was your grandmother who taught you to surround each day with prayer and had an intimacy with God that was both beautiful and contagious. Perhaps it was a layperson in your church, or a neighbor in your community who was always looking for the next person to help and the next social ill to ameliorate.

We know that our initial sources for learning about God are our parents. Through them we learn early on about trust and love and consistency; through them we learn powerful and lasting lessons about how friendly the world is and how easy (or hard) it is to survive. Through our parents we learn about creation *and* its Creator, as well as about ourselves and our value in the grand scheme of things.

If we are fortunate enough to have parents who take us to church when we are young, we may begin to know God in a special way through our pastor. I recently codirected an elementary church camp with my sister. One day during lunch I was told by a camper who had just finished third grade that for the longest time ("when I was little") he thought that his pastor was God. When he went to church and saw that the pastor was there he would say to his parents "God is in today." This camper was voicing a profound truth, for in a very real way, the pastor of the church is Christ's ordained representative on earth. And although it is equally true to say that all Christians are Christ's representatives in the world, there is a distinction to be made between laity and clergy.

By virtue of the education, training, supervision, and evaluation that precede ordination, clergy become the church's representative ministers in a special way. In a later chapter I will discuss the difference between being called to general ministry and to representative ministry. Suffice it to say here that from the birth of the church, those who are set apart for representative ministry have been viewed as people with especially close ties to God through Christ. Needless to say, that closeness does not make them better or more valuable human beings. It does, however, serve to potentially draw their congregants closer to God.

Think back over the years to pastors you have known. What did they teach you about the joys of spending a lifetime in service to others in the name of Jesus Christ? Were they outgoing and friendly or quiet and reserved? Were they good preachers who seemed to radiate the love of God with every word or did they convey more uncertainty and doubt than faith? What kind of a public stance did they take against injustice, and how did they inspire others to do the same? How important did you feel when you were with them? Were they happy and content, or were they restless and burdened by sorrows? What did they teach you about the day-to-day work of the ordained pastor and what it is like to be in ordained ministry? Is there anything in them that you want to emulate in your own life?

When a student told his dad that he was thinking seriously about becoming a pastor himself, his dad told him that if he could do anything else he should do it. The father did not mean to discourage the student or talk him out of his pursuit. Rather he was telling him that ministry is hard work across the years, full of joy but also full of sorrow. It is a tremendous responsibility to be con-

I don't agree

cerned with the care of souls, and the daily work of leading others to "do justice, and to love kindness, and to walk humbly with . . . God" (Micah 6:8) can be a heavy and lonely burden to bear.

Such work requires intense and thorough preparation. It requires intimate knowledge of God and oneself, along with openness to others and willingness to be proved wrong and to change. It requires a flexibility and humility of spirit, an intellectual curiosity about the world, and a healthy sense of humor all at the same time. And it requires a love of God and God's creation that is as wide as the sky and as deep as the ocean.

A very wise rabbi told me shortly before I was due to give birth to our first child that when the baby was born and forever after I would know the highest highs and the lowest lows it is possible to know. Such was the landscape of parenthood. In the thirteen years since my friend made that prediction I have found the truth of his words over and over again. I have found similar highs and lows in ministry as well.

It is a great privilege to serve others in Christ's name and to have such ready access to people. Clergy are called upon at times of great celebration and great sadness, of great joy and great sorrow, of decision making and reconciliation. They are present by invitation and expectation at all of the great crossroads of life. They are looked to for leadership in facing society's ills head-on with courage and grace and for inspiration for others to do the same. No other professional is as welcomed and expected to drop by unannounced for a visit at home or in the hospital. No other professional is expected to be willing to face and wrestle with life's biggest questions and challenges with courage and wisdom and to walk fearlessly with others to the edges of this life while helping them to make their peace with God.

THE TASKS OF MINISTRY

Clergy are concerned about the health and well-being of their congregation as a living, breathing, effective witness for Jesus Christ in the world. The multiple roles of the ordained pastoral leader require a vision that is clear and realistic yet flexible.

Ordained leaders are called to be pastors, priests, prophets, and administrators. Often these roles complement each other; sometimes they are in conflict. They are present in the expectations of the church and the parishioners; they are always called for in response to a broken and needy world.

In the classic text *Preface to Pastoral Theology*, Seward Hiltner looks at three different aspects of the pastoral office: healing, sustaining, and guiding. Hiltner writes:

> "Healing" in this connection means binding up wounds in the precise sense of the good-Samaritan story. "Sustaining" means "comforting" in the original sense of "with courage," upholding or standing with one who suffers even if the situation cannot be altered except perhaps by change in the person's attitude. "Guiding" within the perspective of shepherding means helping to find the paths when that help has been sought.[2]

Communicating the gospel both to those within the faith and those not in the faith community is a vitally important part of the pastoral office.

> As interrelated aspects of the function of communicating the gospel, therefore, we can accept: (1) learning, understanding, or instructing; (2) realizing, deepening, or edifying; and (3) celebrating, reminding, or commemorating.[3]

Organizing the fellowship of the church includes:

> (1) nourishing, feeding, or aiding its development; (2) protecting or purifying from threats within or without it; (3) relating it, positively or negatively, to other bodies such as institutions, cultures, or states. All of these aim at the organic wholeness, integrity, and welfare of the fellowship; but each is dominantly relevant in a different kind of situation.[4]

In these perspectives Hiltner shows the range of skills and sensibilities necessary in one who is ordained. To focus on one aspect of ministry, such as preaching, to the neglect of other aspects means that the church will be weakened. A pastor who puts the majority of time into preparation for preaching and who fails to visit members will risk preaching irrelevant sermons because he will be out of touch with people's concerns, joys, and sorrows. Such a pastor will become a threat to the organization as people feel increasingly neglected.

Likewise, the pastor who concentrates on pastoral care and counseling to the neglect of her own personal study and devotional time and disregards the administrative structure of the church may be beloved by the congregants but will run the risk of not offering informed leadership that results in the moving along of the vision of the church. Without careful and ongoing attention to the infrastructure of the church, it will become vulnerable.

Another way to view the pastoral office is to look at the different aspects of work the pastor does routinely. This work can be divided into the following four areas:

adequate?

1. Communication and Education
2. Caring and Reconciliation
3. Administration and Organization
4. Theology and Ethics[5]

The Communication and Education aspects of ministry include the many ways that pastors teach the body of material that forms the corpus of the Judeo-Christian heritage. Their teaching and preaching of scripture, doctrine, and theology of the church is accomplished in many ways, some more obvious than others. On Sunday morning, for example, it is clear when the pastor is leading worship and teaching a class that the communicative and educative aspects of ministry are in the ascendancy. It is also the case, however, that when the pastor begins each meeting with a prayer, or gives leadership to the building of an affordable housing complex in town, that he or she is likewise teaching a lifestyle that is consistent with the gospel and being prophetic about the Christian's responsibility to others who may be less materially fortunate. Teaching, preaching, and prophecy, then, are included in the communication and education aspects of ordained ministry.

When the pastor is visiting in homes or hospitals, counseling troubled families or individuals, or helping couples think about marriage within the Christian context, the caring and reconciliation aspects of ministry are predominant. These situations are, of course, obvious ones in relationship to this aspect of ministry. Making sure that meetings have agendas and therefore are not meandering exercises of endurance is also an expression of care.

In my many years at Drew I have heard very few students say that they looked forward to the administration that is so much a part of the pastoral office. In response I have tried to help students see that behind every piece of paper there is a person.

When I was seriously ill some years ago a woman in my church wrote to tell me that members of the church wanted to help my family in any way they could. They offered to cook meals, do laundry, help with child care, and clean the house. The writer of the note asked me to please let them help us in these ways and to allow her to "organize the love." I have never heard a better definition for administration than the one Mrs. Lorraine Giffin gave me in that note. The administrative and organizational aspects of ministry do just that. They are the myriad ways in which the pastor sets about to "organize the love" of the gospel evidenced in that particular congregation. Preparing reports and bulletins are obvious examples of these aspects. Taking time to see that the right people are in key leadership roles and that segments of the congregation do not feel neglected and disenfranchised are also related to these aspects, which protect the body "from threats within and without" by helping the organization to remain healthy and whole.

Finally, the theological and ethical aspects of the pastor's work are evident throughout all of the above. We are called to be theologians and ethicists everywhere we go. The truth of this is easily seen when we are called upon to help a family think about the withdrawal of life support from a loved one who is terminally ill or when we help a young unmarried woman wrestle with whether or not she will have an abortion. We are also theologians and ethicists, however, when we make up our visitation list, work to put together the annual budget, and follow through on the details of the newsletter. In everything we do our theology can be seen. Everything we do shows our deepest ethical decisions about how we will treat people and what our values and priorities are in light of the gospel of Jesus Christ. The question is not, Will I be a theologian and ethicist when I am a pastor? The question is instead, What kind of theology and ethics will my ministry reflect?

THE LIFE OF SERVICE: HIGHS AND LOWS

Having read the above paragraphs about the nature and work of the ordained pastoral leader, stop and ask yourself what your reaction is. Do you find yourself eager to engage in this kind of work? Can you imagine yourself preaching Sunday after Sunday with a word from the Lord for your people? Do you want to spend your days and your nights thinking about ways to help your people fall more deeply in love with God and become more faithful to God's claim upon their lives? Are you ready to face the conflicts that will inevitably arise within the church over things that may not seem important to you but may threaten to split the congregation? How do you feel about working with budgetary processes, and how easily are you able to see that budgets are ethical exercises as well as fiscal ones? Do you long to visit your people, counsel them, and offer them God's grace liturgically and every way you can?

As my student's father asked him, I ask you: Is there anything else you could do with your life? Ministry is a rewarding and demanding vocation. It requires considerable physical, emotional, intellectual, and spiritual energy. To be an effective pastor one must stay fit on every level, remain curious and intellectually alive, be willing to do the ongoing work of self-reflection in order to offer authentic and helpful leadership, and maintain a spiritually disciplined life.

Ministry requires a willingness on the part of the ordained leader to go where most other people would not go: into valleys of grief that threaten to overwhelm the human spirit and undermine faith; into the parts of the human spirit where hate and hopelessness and anger and prejudice reside. It requires a healthy ego, courage in the face of great evil in its many forms, and a dedication to routing it out in the name of Jesus Christ. It requires fearless self-examination and a willingness to change when patterns of relating are revealed to be unhealthy and unwise. It requires a willingness to love the unlovable, accept the unacceptable, forgive the unforgivable. In short, it requires a wisdom and a love and a grace that can come only from God, and therefore, above all else, it requires the ordained one to be in constant communion with the Source of all joy, the Giver of every good and perfect gift, the

Morning Star of all hope, the Counselor of all justice, the Alpha and Omega of all peace.

We live in a time of unparalleled opportunity and of technological advance that allows us to extend the life span and to make instantaneous connections across the globe through our home and office computers. Ministry today requires its ordained leaders to be current in their knowledge of societal trends and issues so that they can be out in front offering insights relevant to further technological and sociological developments and offering leadership that will result in a more just and compassionate society. Pastors must be well read across disciplinary lines and understand, as the great theologian Richard Niebuhr did, that when they climb into the pulpit they must do so with a Bible in one hand and a newspaper in the other.

The pastor who is consistently doing all of this will often feel as if there is always more work to be done and never enough hours in the day. The work of ministry requires long, often lonely hours. It involves interruptions of family time and personal study time. And it offers countless opportunities for pastors to feel as if the seeds that they are sowing in the name of Jesus Christ are falling on rocky ground with no hope of bearing fruit. At the same time it requires pastors to know the importance of maintaining balance and boundaries in their lives by taking regular time off for rest and recreation without feeling guilty. Such a discipline is not an easy one, and all too many pastors end up failing to take time for themselves away from the demands of ministry.

There are many times, however, when the rewards of ministry far outweigh the difficulties. I remember two women, Edith and Sally. Edith was a young woman in her early forties whom I first met when I was a hospital chaplain. She was in the hospital suffering with breast cancer. I was called to her bedside by the nurse because Edith had voiced the wish to throw herself out the second story window. Within minutes after I arrived at Edith's room, she was sitting next to me with her head on my shoulder crying uncontrollably over her great loss. She had a husband and two small sons she would be soon leaving, and she could not bear the pain of that knowledge.

Over the next several months I visited Edith frequently. My

heart broke to hear her talk about her children growing up without remembering her. I offered to help her make a tape recording for them, and she immediately said yes. She carefully worked on the letter that she would record, which contained a mother's love and dreams for her sons as well as a voice that they could remember whenever they listened to the tape. In many ways it was her final gift to them, her final act of letting go. Listening to her read that letter while the tape recorder captured her love and hopes and dreams for her children is one of the most difficult acts of ministry I have ever been called upon to perform.

Edith had still more to teach me, however. As we met during the months before her death and talked about God and what had happened to her, she told me that although she had been raised in the church and had always had a vital and lively faith, she had been entirely unable to pray for some time. Over the course of several visits I discovered why. She was angry at God for her cancer and blamed God for taking her from her children and her husband. She was only in her early forties and felt entitled to many more years to live and love and laugh and enjoy her children and her children's children. God had become for her the enemy, the silent wall who did not respond to her agonized pleas for life, the Cosmic Sadist[6] who delighted in her tragedy.

Although I had encountered this theology before, Edith's trouble with prayer was unique. She had been taught that she was not allowed to be angry at God. Furthermore, she believed that if she did become angry at God and happened to die in those moments of anger, she would be consigned to hell for all eternity. Her prior relationship with Jesus Christ did nothing to prevent or remedy that consignment.

When I understood Edith's belief system, I knew why she could not pray. If I am angry at someone, it is difficult for me to pretend otherwise. It is also difficult for me to move on in the relationship if that anger is not addressed. Burying anger does not help the situation, for the anger only "lies in wait" and contaminates the relationship by slowly poisoning it.

Edith could not pray because she was blocked in her relationship with God. She was more angry than she had ever been, but could not express it. In the process of building a wall around her anger so that God could not see it, she also built a wall around the rest of her feelings for God. Nothing could come through. It was all buried deep inside. To allow anything to surface meant that she risked the eruption of her deep anger, and that would entail risking eternal damnation.

I gently told Edith that I thought she was mistaken about God. I told her about the love of God, which is limitless and quite accepting of us regardless of what we feel or when we feel it. I discovered that she had never read any psalms and pointed her to several psalms of lament that were quite open in their disappointment and anger at God. I asked her to read them before I came back to visit her. She was amazed to discover that people of the Bible were at times quite angry with God. That their writings were legitimated in the Bible meant that their feelings were legitimated as well. Because theirs were, hers were also. She began to believe it was safe for her to be honest with God about all she was feeling. She began to tell God how angry she was, and was surprised and delighted to discover that the earth did not shake when she did so.

I remember one particular time when I did nothing but listen to her cry and rail against God for causing her cancer to take her from her children and husband whom she loved so very much. When her anger was spent, she found that she needed God desperately, and it was as if she came rushing into God's arms as a child does after being reconciled to a parent. She slept more soundly that night than she had in months.

I remain grateful to this day that I was able to help Edith at that point in her life. She was estranged from the very source of comfort she needed, the only One to whom she could turn for final healing and victory over her despair.

I first met Sally when she was in the junior high youth group of the church in which I was the student assistant while in seminary. She was a delightful young woman full of promise and life. Sally went away to college and then moved to another part of the country when she was offered her first job. She met Tim and quickly fell in love with him. Their relationship progressed nicely for the most part, with the usual struggles that are a part of a couple becoming committed to each other and establishing patterns of relating. Sally would call me once in a while to tell me how they were doing. I wondered silently if they would last as a couple because their families were from different cultural backgrounds although they both grew up in this country. Tim's parents immigrated to the United States when his older brother was born. They retained close ties with their homeland and returned there frequently to see relatives and ensure that their children would know their heritage. Each set of parents had a good marriage patterned after the culture and families from which they came.

As is often the case, Tim and Sally had different expectations of what their marriage would be like, about what roles each one would play relative to child rearing and the financial realities of their family life. They were by nature and temperament quite different people. Sally made no choice without examining all options thoroughly and slowly; Tim preferred to make quick decisions, basing them on what felt right at the moment. They had ample opportunities for disagreement and equally ample opportunities to learn the fine art of compromise.

When they decided to become engaged, they asked me to perform the wedding ceremony. Before I could say a word about premarital counseling, they said that they did not want to get married until they had several sessions with me to explore together their differences as well as their dreams. Our times together were full of discussion and long silences, smiles and tears. At times they were not certain they would marry; at other times they were overjoyed with the thought of it and eager for their wedding day to come.

Sally and Tim have been married a few years now and are expecting their first child as I write these words. We have kept in touch though they live some distance away. I know that I played a significant part in this young couple's decision to marry and in their ability to communicate effectively with each other.

Is the life of service one to which you feel called? Do you say, as Paul said:

Woe to me if I do not proclaim the gospel? (1 Corinthians 9:16)

In this passage of scripture Paul is talking about his need to preach the gospel. In a paradoxical way, he was both free to walk away from the life of preaching Christ crucified, dead, and risen and at the same time not free at all. In Jesus Christ he knew the greatest freedom known to humankind. At the same time, he knew bondage to a way of life that was stronger than any chains he was ever bound by in prison. Paul could no more turn away from Christ than he could change the color of his eyes.

This connection to Christ and the meaning and value of his life were one and the same. Paul had found in ministry the highest highs he had every known, and even the difficult times were bracketed by the joy he knew in the close walk with Christ.[7] It is interesting to note that while Paul had in fact suffered a great deal for his faith, he said that the real suffering would begin in his life if he *did not* preach the gospel!

Paul meant that his life would be utterly bereft of meaning without the gospel and the mandate to preach it. He had connected with people in deep and lasting ways, helped them to live lives of integrity and promise, reconciliation and hope. He had helped them live with justice and mercy, to rise above their poverty and social stations and live more abundantly than they ever imagined possible. He had helped them to know that they were loved by God beyond their wildest dreams.

Is that what you want in your own life? If it is, then you have come to the right place to prepare for the life of service. In seminary you will wrestle with angels as you ponder life's biggest questions. You will meet interesting faculty and staff and students who are exciting and diverse. You will daily encounter yourself and wrestle with life's meaning in new ways. Even the difficult times you will have in seminary will be softened by the knowledge that you are walking with God and surrounded by a great cloud of witnesses.

Are you ready to do whatever it takes to prepare yourself for a life of service? Are you ready to commit yourself to the rigors of theological education that are necessary for such ministry? Are you ready to spend long nights reading and writing, long days in discussion and perhaps confusion? Are you ready to have the belief systems you came to seminary with challenged and changed and have yourself changed in the process? Are you ready to wonder in fresh and exciting ways who God is and where you are going? Are you ready to think in new and (perhaps) frightening ways what it *really* means to do justice, to love mercy, and to walk

Can be scary

— 27 —

humbly with God? Are you ready to get to know yourself more intimately than you ever have before? Are you sure this is what you want to do in order to gain greater knowledge about what kind of ministry God is calling you to?

If you are, then read on. In the following chapters I will be asking you to think more carefully about your time in seminary and your preparation for ministry, in order to help you come to some greater clarity about where you are headed in your life and why you are now in seminary.

If your answer to the above questions is "I'm not sure," I hope you will still read on. Be assured that others reading this book have felt similar confusion or uncertainty.

In *Wishful Thinking: A Theological ABC* Frederick Buechner writes with insight about the concept of vocation:

> The kind of work God usually calls you to is the kind of work (a) that you need most to do and (b) that the world most needs to have done...neither the hair shirt nor the soft berth will do. The place God calls you to is the place where your deep gladness and the world's deep hunger meet.[8]

As you read this book and think about your preparation for ministry in this broken and hungry world, this world so full of promise and resources, let yourself wonder about where it is that your deep gladness lies. My prayer for you is that this book will help you discover your deep gladness with greater precision as you learn more about the world's deep hunger while you are in seminary.

EXERCISE

You may find it helpful to do the exercises at the end of each chapter with another seminary student. Sharing the hopes and concerns that will surface through these exercises can help you to feel less isolated and shed light on both the particular and the universal dimensions of your experience.

In the book *Wouldn't Take Nothing for My Journey Now*, Maya Angelou writes:

The New Testament informs the reader that it is more blessed to give than to receive. I have found that among its other benefits, giving liberates the soul of the giver. . . . The giver is as enriched as is the recipient, and more important, that tangible but very psychic force of good in the world is increased.[9]

Take some time now to think about Angelou's observations about the life of charity and service. Do you agree with her or not?

Think next about your models for ministry. Who were the people that first shaped your understanding of what it means to be a Christian in service in the world? What did they teach you about the importance and value of reaching out to others in love and service? What lessons did you learn from them about the nature of ministry and the life of Christian service?

After you have answered these questions, think about the reasons you came to seminary. What do you most want to do with your life? Try to summarize it in one sentence. What excites you most about being in ministry? What do you hope to offer to the world? Finally, take some time to think about your expectations for seminary. What do you hope to learn while you are here? What has you most excited about being here? What has you most concerned?

As you come to the close of your reflections, spend some time in prayer. The following prayer is a starting point. Use it and adapt it as you like. And may God bless you as you continue on the journey.

Prayer: Gracious God, thank you for the witness of all of the saints from the beginning of the church. Thank you especially for those who served as my early models for ministry. Help me to continue to learn from their example and to remain open to new models of ministry that you bring my way. Be with me throughout my seminary journey. May it be a time of blessing and discovery. Use me to bless others as they also seek your direction and will for their lives. In Christ's name I pray. Amen.

CHAPTER 2

Wrestling with Holy Things: Reframing Theological Education

Hey, Mom, once you get the outside frame, it's easy! Russell Cetuk

y son Russ and I were putting together a puzzle of Daniel and the Lion's Den. I was thoroughly enjoying my time alone with Russ, enjoying doing something explicitly "religious." I was talking with Russ about Daniel's faith, the protection of the angel, and how God is always with us. I asked him if he had ever been afraid, as Daniel must have been, and had asked God to help him. His response was a quiet "Yeah, sure, Mom," followed by a sudden outburst: "Hey, Mom, once you get the outside frame, it's easy!"

While Russ was referring to the process of putting the frame of the puzzle together first and only then tackling the harder picture inside, his insight about puzzles is not limited to those that come in a box. It also describes the bigger puzzles of life. As Russ pointed out, looking first at the finished frame around the picture helps us make sense of the heart of the matter. The perspective we have about life's puzzles, to continue with his insight, affects how easily we make all of the pieces fit together.

Although Russ did not know it when he made the observation, he was also talking about theological education as an enterprise, as you will no doubt soon discover. In no other educational process are there so many varied puzzle pieces in need of arrangement. While you are in seminary you will be confronted with challenges on every level. You will be asked to consider life's biggest questions and be challenged to become a leader who will assist others to wrestle with those questions for themselves. You will be pressed to renegotiate the substance of your own faith commitments based on the insights of the same academy that may at times seem to be faith's adversary.

You may have come to theological school expecting to be able to navigate your seminary experience with your present faith stance. You no doubt have come expecting to find help and encouragement in the deepening of that faith. Indeed, it is a crucial part of your formation as a spiritual leader to "give regular attendance upon the private and public worship of God,"[1] and you probably expect (rightfully so) your theological school to be arranged to that end. In other words, you come expecting the "outside frame" around your seminary experience to be designed to support deeper explorations of your faith and to sustain you in the process.

That you have come with the desire to deepen your own faith commitments means that you are foreseeing the realities of your future work with clarity. For how will you know to point people to the Source of every good and perfect gift, as they celebrate life's blessings and ponder their good fortune, if you are out of touch with that Source? From where will you draw courage to face evil in its many forms if you do not know the One who said "Take courage; I have conquered the world" (John 16:33)? And what will sustain you during those long, lonely, difficult days of ministry if you do not have a deep and habitual spiritual life from which to draw as one draws a drink from a deep well on a hot day?

Unfortunately, many theological schools in the moderate to liberal Protestant tradition seem not to be structured in such a way as to assist or promote students' personal spiritual formation. Rather, the internal (sometimes unconscious) confusion over whether schools are properly understood as seminaries or as schools of religion has contributed to a "hands-off" view relative to inquiry about and support for students' personal practice of the spiritual disciplines.[2]

In her discussion of contemporary higher education, Sharon Parks notes that the prevailing model is built on the assumptions of Western epistemology. She writes:

> The phenomenal can be known, but noumenal reality cannot; and if it cannot, the reasoning goes, then questions of meaning, morality, ultimacy, and faith stand outside the realm of knowledge and are beyond (or irrelevant to) the concerns of the academy....Further, the knowledge of the "object" that is known has been divorced from its relationship to the "subject" who knows, thus diminishing the significance of emotion, intuition, the personal and the complexity emerging from the practice of lived experience (domains difficult to apprehend empirically).[3]

Parks's assessment accurately describes the pedagogical dualism lurking in some theological schools, particularly in the moderate to liberal Protestant tradition. This dualism is being challenged today by several pedagogies and theologies that proclaim experience a worthy teacher. Feminist, womanist, process, and liberation theologies; Clinical Pastoral Education, supervised ministry/field education; and the resurgence of interest across denominational lines in small groups as a way to shepherd group members to deeper faith commitments, to name a few, all have lived experience as their basis. The old dichotomy, however, between the classical academic disciplines and what is increasingly called "pastoral theology" still exists, and it will exert pressure on you to deny the importance of your experience. To return to Russ's insight about puzzles and frames, the predominant frame in many theological schools seems to be that of intellectual development only.

For example, you may learn about critical methods of reading and exegeting scripture without being asked to talk about the implications of the same scripture for your own life and your ministry in the world. At the same time, the deconstructive nature of the curriculum's substance may seem like a steady attack on your faith. I have known many students who wonder who God is and question the divinity of the man Jesus, who question what if anything is to be taken literally in the Bible, and who become afraid that their tenuous faith will be eroded beyond repair as long as they are in seminary.

The dilemma of the special nature of theological education and its location in the academy and the church has long been noted. In the classic study of theological education by H. Richard Niebuhr, *The Purpose of the Church and Its Ministry*, we read:

> If students are not personally involved in the study of theology they are not yet studying theology at all but some auxiliary science such as the history of ideas or ancient documents. Hence theological study is hazardous; the involvement may become so personal and emotional that intellectual activity ceases and the work of abstraction, comparison and criticism stops. Other hazards appear because intellectual activity requires that the objects of ultimate concern in the study be often set at the fringe of awareness while ideas and patterns, forms and relations are put in the center.... The point to be insisted on here is that the theological community is constituted not

by teachers and learners but by these and the subjects of their common inquiry.[4]

Niebuhr is correct about the constituents of the theological community. Because you are a member of this community it is imperative that you discover and discuss the impact of your intellectual growth upon your spiritual growth and vice versa. You will need help to discern how what Evelyn Underhill calls your "correspondence with the spiritual environment" is being challenged and enriched. Underhill describes the gradual shift in one's vision as this correspondence develops:

> The horizon is widened, our experience is enormously enriched, and at the same time our responsibilities are enlarged...and as a result, first our notions about life, our scale of values, begins to change, and then we do.[5]

You will find that the spiritual landscape that Underhill refers to will be constantly changing for you while you are in seminary, for the reality of theological education is such that you will be addressing God on a daily basis in a variety of ways. This sustained exposure to God and the implications of such an encounter mean that you will be confronted with yourself and your values and beliefs in life changing ways. The reverberations from such an encounter with the Divine have long been noted in the annals of human experience. Jacob's all-night match with the angel (Genesis 32:24-32) dramatically exemplifies how we are affected when we dare to touch holy things. Jacob's name was changed, and he limped after the encounter. Likewise, in theological education, you will find your self-understanding dramatically altered through the seminary experience, and you may at times feel as if you are limping along after you encounter God in a new way.

Some faculty fail to appreciate the deconstructive nature of theological education and its impact on the participants. That means that sometimes students fail to learn all that they might while in seminary. You may also find, if you are not careful, that you are viewing the faculty as the adversary; this unfortunate view will further undermine the educational process, as well as your future ministry. I have had all too many conversations with students whose primary goal had become graduating with some shred of faith intact while somehow satisfying the requests of the faculty in fulfilling curricular requirements. What some students fail to see is that the faculty are not the enemy; rather they are midwives of sorts, helping students through a difficult labor so that a newer, deeper faith informed by the intellectual gifts of the tradition can be born.

REFRAMING THEOLOGICAL EDUCATION

My recognition of the kind of confusion I saw in these students, and many others as well, has led to this book. Russ recognized the frame's importance for getting the rest of the picture. Indeed, the frame makes all the difference in how we see the rest of the picture. The right frame can enhance the picture, bringing out subtle differences in shading, highlighting certain aspects of the picture, and allowing us to focus on details we might miss otherwise. I believe that, in spite of the difficulties present in much of contemporary Protestant theological education, it is possible to develop a love of learning and critical analysis while at the same time deepening your personal faith commitments.

You will be helped throughout your seminary career if you learn to reframe your view of theological education from that of intellectual development only to the larger frame of spiritual formation in a self-conscious, rationally disciplined, and committed way. We turn our attention now to a discussion of the nature of the process of *reframing* and a theological understanding of the same. In order to understand the concept of reframing, you should first consider the role your own perspective has in experience. "One person's candy is another person's poison" suggests how our perspective on a given issue or event is peculiar to each of us. That humankind tends to equate and confuse *perspective* with *reality* has been noted since ancient times. As early as the first century A.D. the philosopher Epictetus offered this corrective: "It is not the things themselves which trouble us, but the opinions that we have about these things." William Shakespeare offered a similar observation, "There is nothing either good or bad, but thinking makes it so."

It is the most natural thing in the world to assume that the way I see things is the way they really are and also the way they ought to be seen by everyone else. Such a view lends itself nicely to a sort of gentle narcissistic arrogance[6] that results in a blindness to other perspectives and ways of being. Paul Watzlawick offers a corrective in his book *The Language of Change: Elements of Therapeutic Communication*:

> Let us remember: We never deal with reality per se, but rather with images of reality—that is, with interpretations. While the number of potentially possible interpretations is very large, our world image usually permits us to see only one—and this *one* therefore appears to be the only possible, reasonable, and permitted solution, and if we don't succeed at first we try and try again—or in other words, we resort to the recipe of doing *more of the same.*[7]

Because of the day-to-day grind of classes and assignments and stresses in other areas of their lives, students sometimes develop a psychological and intellectual myopia of sorts as a defense. Content on "just getting through," they often miss the opportunities for spiritual growth along the way. What is called for is a new way of seeing the seminary experience. It needs to be reframed so that it can be befriended and claimed *in toto* as self-conscious spiritual formation.

Watzlawick and others define the process of reframing in the following way:

> To reframe, then, means to change the conceptual and/or emotional setting or viewpoint in relation to which a situation is experienced and to place it in another frame which fits the "facts" of the same concrete situation equally well or even better, and thereby changes its entire meaning.[8]

The authors cite an example from their work with clients: A man with a very bad stammer became a salesman. This position quite understandably deepened his lifelong concern about this speech defect. Instead of viewing his predicament negatively, as would have been so easy, he was invited to view it positively, since it would prevent the rapid-fire, nonstop, annoying barrage salesmen often utilize to "make the sale." The salesman, in contrast, would be able to enlist the help and support of those he was pitching to since they would most likely listen patiently and carefully as people usually do to someone who stammers. The therapist asked him whether he had ever considered what an unusual advantage his handicap could become in his new occupation.

Likewise, when I began my first unit of Clinical Pastoral Education (CPE) upon graduating from seminary, I realized to my chagrin that as part of the program I would be on duty at the hospital for an entire weekend. That meant that from Friday night until Monday morning I would be called when a chaplain was needed. I felt totally unprepared and wholly inadequate for this challenge. Nevertheless, when it was my turn for weekend duty, my supervisor handed me the beeper at 5:00 P.M. that Friday afternoon with a slow smile spreading across his face. I mumbled something about not being up to the task. He responded by exclaiming, "What a great opportunity for learning!" and promptly left the office. As I recall that weekend, it was one of repeated crises and little sleep. I thought often of my supervisor's words. In all honesty, they did not help me then to feel more confident and better able to respond to the drama of human suffering I saw up close that weekend. In subsequent months and years, however, I appreciated my supervisor's wisdom; that weekend and the encounters that followed it were indeed great opportunities for learning. He had helped me to successfully reframe my approach to CPE. He invited me to remove the frame made out of my fears and self-doubts and to replace it with a frame made out of hope and anticipation. While the heart of the picture remained constant, my view of it changed. I came to see the challenges of CPE (and other areas of my life) not as assaults on my worthiness but as invitations to growth.

I offer one final example from *The Adventures of Tom Sawyer*. When faced with the prospect of spending Saturday afternoon whitewashing Aunt Polly's fence instead of having fun like all the other boys, Tom sank into despair over the work and the ridicule he was sure to suffer at the hands of passersby. Suddenly Tom was seized by an inspiration when the very boy, of all boys, whose ridicule he had most feared happened by:

"Hello, old chap, you got to work, hey?"
"Why it's you, Ben! I warn't noticing."

"Say—I'm going a'swimming, I am. Don't you wish you could? But of course you'd druther work wouldn't you? Course you would!"
Tom contemplated the boy a bit, and said:
"What do you call work?"
"Why, ain't that work?"
Tom resumed his whitewashing, and answered carelessly:
"Well, maybe it is, and maybe it ain't. All I know is it suits Tom Sawyer."
"Oh come, now, you don't mean to let on that you like it?"
The brush continued to move.
"Like it? Well, I don't see why I oughn't to like it. Does a boy get a chance to whitewash a fence every day?"
That put things in a new light. Ben stopped nibbling his apple. Tom swept his brush daintily back and forth—stepped back to note the effect—added a touch here and there—criticized the effect again—Ben watching every move and getting more and more interested, more and more absorbed.
Presently he said:
"Say, Tom, let *me* whitewash a little."

By the end of the afternoon, Tom had succeeded in getting his friends to pay him for the privilege of painting the fence. He had not only successfully avoided the tedium of whitewashing, he had money to show for it, thereby proving himself to be a master at reframing!

REFRAMING IN SCRIPTURE AND BONHOEFFER

Reframing offers a conceptual tool that helps us see our experience in a different light. When looked at from a theological perspective, we see that reframing is at its heart an opportunity for spiritual growth in keeping with the gospel message. In its entirety the gospel is a message about change and release from former ways of living and being and understanding life. Jesus of Nazareth was the agent of that change. He reframed our understanding of God when he referred to God as "Abba" and invited us to do the same.[9] One's relationship with the Almighty came from the love in one's heart. Jesus offered a radical challenge to the assumption that salvation could be earned by one's own efforts. What mattered instead was the scope and intensity of one's love. In response to the lawyer's question about the greatest law, Jesus said:

" 'You shall love the Lord your God with all your heart, and with all your soul, and with all your mind.' This is the greatest and first commandment. And a second is like it: 'You shall love your neighbor as yourself.' On these two commandments hang all the law and the prophets." (Matthew 22:37-40)

Jesus' summary of all the law and the prophets pointed to the reality that it was possible to act in accordance with the law without necessarily being filled with the love of God. In the Synoptic Gospels (Matthew, Mark, and Luke) we read the story of the rich young ruler who comes to Jesus immediately after Jesus blessed the little children. Perhaps he was watching the children with Jesus and saw their sheer delight in being with him and being alive. Something prompted him to examine his own life and wonder about it. All three Gospel writers tell us that he approached Jesus as soon as Jesus was finished talking with the children. I particularly like Mark's Gospel (Mark 10:17-22) because it so beautifully paints a picture of a young man eager to learn about life:

> As he was setting out on a journey, a man ran up and knelt before him, and asked him, "Good Teacher, what must I do to inherit eternal life?"

After Jesus told him that he should obey the commandments, the young man replied that he had done so all of his life. Jesus then told him, having apparently sized him up as being spiritually immature, that he must do one more thing, the hardest thing of all. Jesus challenged him to go beyond the law and to empty himself of his attachments to the world by selling his possessions, giving them to the poor and following Jesus thereafter. Such a radical action could only come if the young man were full of the love of God in a profound and life-changing way. The young man had apparently lived a righteous life, but it was a life in which he was too focused on himself and in which he lacked charity and love for his neighbor. In order for him to really live on this side of the grave and on the other side, he needed the transformation and rebirth Jesus Christ offered in his very person.

Speaking with authority in the Sermon on the Mount, Jesus again and again challenged the prevailing wisdom and customs, and pushed his hearers to see the world in a different way. Six times he said, "You have heard that it was said...but I say to you..." Through these sayings he invited the listener to understand the world and relationships in a new way. Whereas the old way involved rigid boundaries between people, which could not be overcome and which served to support the social order of the day, the new ways of living had reconciliation, fidelity, and forgiveness at their heart. Such a radically different worldview was at the core of Jesus' reframed message of hope and life. The picture in the frame, God's love, had not changed. What had changed was the way God's children were enabled to live with and love each other and the way that reconciliation and forgiveness was possible in a new way through Jesus Christ.

Faith in God through Christ enables one to see anew the world and the circumstances of one's life; *they are reframed.* This same faithful relationship with God across time enables us to withstand the trials and difficulties that come our way and to mature sufficiently to view them as opportunities and not obstacles to an abundant life. It is the mature faith that is able to do as Paul instructs in 1 Thessalonians 5:18: "Give thanks in all circumstances; for this is the will of God in Christ Jesus for you."

This mind-set of thanksgiving is not an easy one to obtain or maintain, however, for students in theological schools. What my rabbi friend said about parenthood applies to students in seminary as well: you will know highs and lows while there. The seminary experience is a stress-filled but exciting one. Most students I have known have enjoyed the study of scripture, the exploration of social issues, the soul searching called for in the process, and the development of ministerial skills and identity that are all at the heart of the formation process in seminary.

At the same time opportunities to despair abound in seminary, and there are never enough hours in the day. Sometimes students entering seminary experience changes in their friendships, in their families, and within themselves at alarming rates. In the face of such a radical departure from the safety of former lives and webs of support, students often begin to wonder at what price they are answering the call to ministry. Some question if it is worth it at all.

If you reach the point of such soul searching and questioning you will be wondering about the cost of discipleship. A second-year student said: "Sometimes that you believe at all is a testimony. Sometimes you have to crawl over, through, and around your life to have faith." This particular student was tired of the struggle, tired of the demands of the classroom, the strains of being a part of a diverse community, the grind of a rather lengthy commute, the pain of separation from family and friends who did not understand her decision to enter seminary. She had given up much to come to Drew and was asking if seminary was worth the sacrifices being asked of her.

Many seminary students know this despair at one time or another. I have found that the confusion that precedes this despair is almost universal. If you find yourself in this confused and questioning state, I invite you to see your confusion as the potential pathway to deeper faith. The classic text *The Cost of Discipleship* by Dietrich Bonhoeffer can help you at this point.

The powerful witness Bonhoeffer gave in the face of the Nazi reign of terror and persecution can serve as a model for theological students today. Bonhoeffer understood that to be a Christian meant that one would suffer, because being a Christian put the believer at odds with the world and its values.

> The cross is laid on every Christian. The first Christ-suffering which every man [and woman] must experience is the call to abandon the attachments of this world.... Thus it begins; the cross is not the terrible end to an otherwise godfearing and happy life, but it meets us at the beginning of our communion with Christ. When Christ calls a man, he bids him come and die.[10]

In many ways Bonhoeffer has captured the essence of what it *should* mean to be in a Protestant theological school today. Challenged as they are, students begin to see their old ways of being in the world as inadequate. Cling as they might to those old patterns and beliefs, they must move beyond them if they are to offer mature spiritual leadership in the future.

In Bonhoeffer's words, they must "come and die." His understanding of what it means to be a Christian came from his theology of the cross. To be a Christian meant that one would suffer and be crucified with Christ. That crucifixion was not to be shunned, but embraced.

To endure the cross is not a tragedy; it is the suffering which is the fruit of an exclusive allegiance to Jesus Christ. When it comes, it is not an accident, but a necessity. It is not the sort of suffering which is inseparable from this mortal life, but the suffering which is an essential part of the specifically Christian life. (98)

Sometimes students in seminary experience first hand the rejection and suffering Bonhoeffer links to the cross. Some students feel family and friends pulling away from them, and the easy rapport they once had with others before going to seminary is often gone. The pain they feel from this and other changes is rightly labeled "suffering."

Many of the students coming to mainline Protestant theological schools come from churches not steeped in this understanding of the difference between the natural and the Christian existence; they do not expect to suffer and are surprised and overwhelmed when they do in the course of their theological education. They have either forgotten the words of Jesus or failed to understand them in the first place:

If any want to become my followers, let them deny themselves and take up their cross and follow me. For those who want to save their life will lose it, and those who lose their life for my sake will find it. (Matthew 16:24-25)

Attempts to save the lives they knew before coming to theological school prove fruitless. Their relationships, their values, their dreams and plans all come under review in the course of their studies. The review itself can be exhilarating and joyful, exhausting and painful all at once. Often the results of this review are such that students discover that they must make changes because the former ways of being are inadequate and must be replaced. The acknowledgment of the need for change and the process of change are often difficult and treacherous; and yet they are also part of the way of the cross—what is meant by the summons, "Come and die."

The Cost of Discipleship, first published in 1937, was a powerful attack on the easy Christianity of the German Lutheran Church at the time. In it Bonhoeffer examined the serious implications of believing in Christ and the intensity of the struggle in humankind's deepest self between the world and God in the face of the call to true discipleship. Although written for another audience, it has much to say to those who would be Christians today and has particular relevance for those who will provide leadership in the Christian church.

The easy Christianity Bonhoeffer denounced subscribed to what he called "cheap grace." Cheap grace was the assurance that the Christian was saved without any corresponding demands being placed on that Christian relative to the way life ought to be lived. It was embraced by those who did not expect to make any real changes in their lives following their commitment to Christ. Rather, they simply expected to have their sins covered without any need to have them excised through a faithful and close walk with God. The subscribers to that kind of Christianity did not expect to suffer for their faith. As Bonhoeffer noted, those embracing cheap grace say in effect:

> I can therefore cling to my bourgeois secular existence, and remain as I was before, but with the added assurance that the grace of God will cover me. (54)

Bonhoeffer understood the embracing of cheap grace to be the death knell of genuine Christianity. He critiqued the Lutheran Church of his day for offering "that which was holy to the scornful and unbelieving" and said that "the call to follow Jesus in the narrow way was hardly ever heard" (58). Cheap grace had boomeranged in the collapse of the organized Church. Given the subsequent events in Nazi Germany and the church's silence when confronted with those evils, we may conclude that Bonhoeffer was a man of vision who saw clearly the trouble ahead for his country and church.

He contrasted cheap grace with costly grace, the real offering of God through Jesus Christ. God's grace "is costly because it costs a [person] his [or her] life, and it is grace because it gives a man the only true life" (47). Such grace involved some effort on the part of the disciple who earnestly sought to follow Christ and love God with all the heart, soul, strength, and mind the disciple had. It necessarily involved the recognition that one's life would come under constant review and change in the daily walk with God. Such review and change would at times be difficult and quite likely painful, but necessary and redeemed nonetheless, for costly grace is the "sanctuary of God" (48) and is "like water on parched ground, comfort in tribulation, freedom from the bondage of a self-chosen way, and forgiveness of all...sins" (52).

Returning to Russ's metaphor, we can say that Bonhoeffer reframed the Christian life from one of ease to one of dissatisfaction with the status quo, from a life of security and comfort to a life whose only comfort was to be found in the challenge of the cross of Jesus Christ and the ultimate shouldering of the same cross by the disciple. While Bonhoeffer's clarion call to discipleship was startling in its attack on the church, it was not new in its substance. The forerunners of his understanding of grace and the effects of the daily walk with God are found in the Gospels and in the church's doctrines.

Throughout the Gospels, we hear of the radical reorientation required of one who would be a Christian:

"Very truly, I tell you, no one can see the kingdom of God without being born from above." (John 3:3)

"Again I tell you, it is easier for a camel to go through the eye of a needle than for someone who is rich to enter the kingdom of God. " (Matthew 19:24)

"If any want to become my followers, let them deny themselves and take up their cross and follow me. For those who want to save their life will lose it, and those who lose their life for my sake, and for the sake of the gospel, will save it." (Mark 8:34-35)

The doctrines of justification through Jesus Christ and sanctification as the process by which a soul over time becomes conformed to God (in John Wesley's terms, "goes on to perfection") have as their basis the doctrine of sin that proclaims that left to our own devices we will continually stray from God. These doctrines also assume that, because of the sinful nature of humankind, the disciple must expect to change.

Although it might be argued that seminary students ought to come expecting, or perhaps even hoping, to be changed by their studies in significant and substantial ways, many do not. You will meet people in seminary who expect to be supported in the faith they came to seminary with and who do not expect to be challenged to change. You will also know students who do expect to change while in seminary, but to do so without the level of challenge and upheaval that is the necessary consequence of a solid program of theological education. Both types of students are at risk, according to Bonhoeffer, for such stasis in the spiritual life is neither healthy nor desirable: "The word of cheap grace has been the ruin of more Christians than any commandment of works" (59). If you are open to spiritual growth, however, then seminary is the place to be! Given the grueling pace of semesters in seminary and their level of intellectual, emotional, and spiritual challenge, you will have the opportunity to make tremendous strides in your spiritual growth and to become open as never before to the costly grace of God through Jesus Christ.

For example, in the stunning confession in 2 Corinthians 12:7-10 we read that Paul was given a "thorn in the flesh" to keep him from "being too elated." After earnest prayer that God would remove the thorn on three occasions, Paul was told that, "My grace is sufficient for you, for power is made perfect in weakness." Thereafter Paul's weighing of strength and weakness became radically different. Whereas before he would celebrate his strength, now he celebrated his weakness. No longer was weakness the enemy; rather it was the avenue through which God's grace could become even more present and active in his life!

> Therefore I am content with weaknesses, insults, hardships, persecutions, and calamities for the sake of Christ; for whenever I am weak, then I am strong. (2 Corinthians 12:10)

Paul celebrated his vulnerability before God and rejoiced that he was weak. By the grace of God, he had reframed the normal understanding of what it means to be weak and what it means to be strong. His weakness was now the source of great joy, for it meant yet another chance to draw closer to God through Christ.

Indeed, scripture abounds with examples of reframing, which is no surprise when the process is understood in theological terms. The essence of reframing is hope, release from captivity to prior ways of understanding and being, solid belief in the right of the individual to be self-determining, and appreciation for the goodness of creation and the capacity of humankind to dream dreams and see visions of a better life. I hope this book helps you reframe your seminary experience and learn to scan the horizon for all the ways that experience can enrich your spiritual life.

Many seminaries today are vitally interested in becoming more inclusive in their faculty and their curriculum. The goal of inclusive theological education—namely, to help students become more aware and appreciative of different modes of thinking and ways of being in the world by exposing them to different cultures, races, ideas, forms of worship, and so forth—parallels the optimism of reframing. It demonstrates that there are multiple ways to be in and view the world.

If you are fortunate enough to be in such a school, the intentionally inclusive nature of the curriculum may well assist you in the process of self-consciously reframing the world in general and your current experience in particular. It should assist you to be more open to befriending what may be the difficult and deeply challenging aspects of theological education.

In a lecture given at Drew Theological School, Dr. Roger Swanson, Director of Evangelism Ministries of The United Methodist Church, said that theological education is not about learning; it is about change. He is correct, of course; it is precisely about changing students' worldviews and receptivity to others; it is about changing their self-understandings in relation to God and others; it is perhaps even about changing their dreams.

Yes, change is an exciting and sometimes fearsome thing, and not something all of us welcome. It takes courage to dare to change and to be open to the One who says, "Behold, I make all things new." I close this chapter, therefore, by turning once again to scripture. I am writing this during Lent, and my mind moves toward what is perhaps the greatest example of reframing ever offered.

I refer to *Good* Friday. This darkest of days, this blemish on the face of history, is the very day that offers unbounded hope to the Christian. This is the day when Jesus would sooner lose his life than lie about God and God's love for us. It is the day when Jesus would sooner beg God's forgiveness for us than abandon us—the day when the earth trembled and the curtain tore because humankind could not bear one moment longer the love offered freely. That we have reframed that awful day and called it "good" is an example of the optimism offered in Christ. It is also, perhaps, the most powerful reminder that God is with us come what may, and that we have nothing to fear for "whether we live or whether we die, we are the Lord's" (Romans 14:8).

EXERCISE

Take a few moments to think about your experience of God that has brought you to enter a program of theological education. Spend some time thinking about your hopes and dreams for your time in seminary. What do you expect will happen to you and for you while you are in your degree program?

How open do you think you are to new experiences and new ideas? Do you generally like the challenge presented by that which is new, or do you generally prefer to remain with that which is known?

Finally, think about the usual ways and means by which you encounter God. Do you easily see God in the experiences of your life and the lives of others? Do you come closer to God through studying or through fellowship? worship? prayer? Do you tend to find God more in the group or privately? To what extent would you describe yourself as being "on the lookout for God"?

You might want to keep a journal in which you note your responses to these questions and other issues raised in this book as a record of your spiritual exploration and growth.

Prayer: Gracious God, you are the source of every good and perfect gift, the fount of every blessing, and you joyously proclaim, "Behold, I make all things new!" I stand on the brink of a new chapter in my life. I have come to a new community to begin a new course of study, and I need your help. Give me eyes and ears to see and hear your will for my life. Help me to be open to the experience of theological education in its entirety so that I may become a new creature in Christ and ever so much better able to serve you because of it. Be with me as I study and make new friends; sustain me when I am tired and weak; lift me above the pressures of this program as you help me to be changed by it. I do so very much want to be the best ministering person I can be, with your help. In Christ's name I pray. Amen.

CHAPTER 3

The Call to Ministry

And he said to them, "Follow me...." Immediately they left the boat and their father, and followed him. Matthew 4:19, 22

s Matthew tells the story of the calling of the first disciples, Peter, Andrew, James, and John did not hesitate to leave all they had and follow Jesus. The Gospel writers disagree about the order in which the disciples were called. They also disagree about the setting of the first call to ministry: Matthew and Mark place it at the Sea of Galilee while Luke places it at the Lake of Gennesaret; John does not say where the call took place. There is one thing that the Gospel writers do agree on, however: without fail those whom Jesus called immediately said, "Yes." Without an apparent thought about the fishing businesses they had worked so hard to establish or the families that depended upon them, they left everything behind and followed Jesus on down the shore. With each step they moved farther and farther away from the people they had been and came closer and closer to becoming the people God had created them to be. As they discovered, to live with Jesus meant by definition that one would change.

Peter, for example, underwent a tremendous transformation while living with Jesus. In the Gospels, early on we see the arrogant Peter who vows his undying allegiance though all else should fail (John 13:37). At the end of John's Gospel we see a different Peter. When Jesus asked Peter if he loved him, Peter responded a quiet "Yes, Lord; you know that I love you." Gone were the boasting and bravado, and in their place was a humble spirit that was born when the cock crowed (John 18).

In the book of Acts we read about Paul's call to ministry and his conversion on the road to Damascus. Known for his prowess in persecuting Christians, Paul met the living Christ while on his way to Damascus to arrest more Christians (Acts 9). His encounter with Christ left him a changed man, on his way to do great things for the Lord. Once converted and called, Paul did not look back—he simply followed the risen Christ.

True discipleship, as Bonhoeffer pointed out, means that the disciple will be at odds with former beliefs and old lifestyles. True discipleship causes us to question our motives as well as our practices; it causes us to become restless with the way things are when justice and mercy are not the order of the day. True discipleship means that when Christ is done with us we will not be the same people we were. True discipleship involves openness to the future and the expectation that we will change as we walk closely with God.

Given the nature of true discipleship it has been interesting and somewhat disconcerting for me to find that by and large seminary students do not come to seminary expecting to change or be changed through the experience. While most expect to leave seminary with more knowledge than they had when they arrived, many students resist the kind of soul searching and wrestling with issues that is part of theological education.

Of course, people entering seminary are no more likely to seek change than the general population. Seminarians come with a variety of theological perspectives and expectations. Some come with the same reluctance to change and the same misunderstanding of the true nature of God's grace that is seen throughout society. Others come expecting and hoping to change and counting on the grace of God to see them through. In short, seminary students are a reflection of humanity.

Considering the realities of today's enrollment patterns, however, one might expect people who decide to become seminary students to have an even greater difficulty given the magnitude of changes wrought in their lives by the decision to enter seminary. When I went to seminary, I was with peers of the same age; most of us had come to seminary three months after graduating from college in our early twenties. We had come with firm convictions about the direction we wanted our professional lives to take; most of us had wanted to be in the ministry at least since adolescence and had not longed for any other kind of work. Few of us had any life experience beyond college life, and most of us had not worked in any jobs besides summer jobs while in college.

This clarity about life's direction coupled with an uninterrupted path into preparation for ministry is not often seen today. The majority of students now come to seminary after leaving first professional careers. That means that many students come having known some satisfaction and dissatisfaction in their lives personally or professionally. They come with conviction about the rightness of their decision because they have known other, less satisfying work prior to enrolling. They are seeking something, and expect to find it in seminary.

Research done by the Association of Theological Schools (ATS) is useful for showing trends in enrollment in theological schools in recent years. A quick look at some of the research illustrates the age diversity of people entering seminary today. The ATS Fact Book for the 1995–1996 academic year reports that the largest percentage of men and women enrolled in theological schools that year were in the 40-49 age range. Furthermore, 58 percent of all enrolled students in ATS schools were 35 years of age or older.[1]

This description was also seen in research done by ATS on the 1994 entering classes in twelve out of the thirteen United Methodist theological schools. From those data we see that at eleven out of the twelve schools, at least half of the entering students were 32 years of age or older.[2] My own school mirrors this data. In 1994, the average age for both male and female students entering Drew Theological School was 40.

In addition to this increase in the average age of students, theological schools have seen a dramatic increase in the number of women attending in the past 25 years. In 1973, ATS reported that 11 percent of all entering students were women. In 1995, the same body reported that 33 percent of all entering students were women.[3] Some schools have a much higher percentage of female students. In 1994, for example, 49 percent of students entering Drew Theological School for all degree programs were women. In the Master of Divinity degree alone (the degree leading to ordination) 55 percent of the entering class were women. Although this percentage is somewhat higher than we have seen for the past several years, women have made up approximately 49 percent of our student body for more than the past decade.

As the above data shows, theological school student bodies today are gender and age inclusive. Some years ago I met with one of our students a few short weeks before she was to graduate.

When she asked me what the mandatory retirement age was in The United Methodist Church, I told her it was 70. Observing her crestfallen expression, I learned that she would soon turn 72! This student was not alone; in fact, she had several contemporaries in the student body at that time.

Such a diversity of age leads to a rich mix within the student body and in classroom discussions. I will comment more on this aspect of the older student in the next chapter. My purpose here in noting this change in makeup of theological schools is simply to point out the corresponding difficulty some students have leaving former lives in order to enter seminary. They often come from established careers and have owned their own homes. Some students move with their families from larger homes into small apartments on campus while others choose to commute long distances in order to avoid such disruptions in family life. Many students wonder how they will pay their own tuition bills alongside those of their college-age children. Unlike the first disciples, many seminary students today do not have such an easy time disengaging from former lives to follow the call.

STUDENTS' REASONS FOR COMING TO SEMINARY

Students come to seminary for a variety of reasons. In the fall of 1994, 794 students entering twelve United Methodist theological schools were asked to respond to a series of questions relative to their entering seminary. One of the questions asked was: "How important were the following in your choice of a profession or calling?" The categories were rated in the following way: 1 = of no importance; 3 = somewhat important; and 5 = very important. The categories and the rate at which they were ranked as being very important were the following:

Experienced a call from God 88%
Desire to serve others 77%
Opportunity for study and growth 75%
Desire to make a difference in the life of the church 71%
Intellectual interest in religious/theological questions 70%

Experience of the community life of a local church 58%
Promise of spiritual fulfillment 57%
Desire to contribute to the cause of social justice 53%
Encouragement of clergy 52%
Experience of pastoral counseling/spiritual direction 43%
Desire to celebrate the sacraments 43%
Search for meaning in life 43%
Influence of family or spouse 33%
Desire to preserve traditions of the church 31%
Influence of friend(s) 23%
Experience in campus Christian organization 16%
A major life event (e.g. a death, divorce) 15%[4]

As the above data show, there are many reasons given for coming to seminary. These reasons are legitimate and believable. My experience of seminary students over the last fifteen years is that they are generally kind and compassionate people who want to make the world a better place and to spread the gospel message of love, justice, and reconciliation. In addition to the reasons stated above, which are the conscious reasons for coming, students enroll in theological degree programs for unconscious reasons as well. These reasons must be discovered and explored while you are in seminary, for they will exert pressure on your ministry in powerful ways unless you are aware of them.

I once was asked to attend the final evaluation session for a student in supervised ministry. His time at the church had been an unsatisfactory one for the supervisor and the lay people on his teaching committee. They had experienced the student as pleasant to be with but lacking energy and enthusiasm for ministry. Despite clear agreements that he would be working in close contact with the people of the church, he spent most of his time working at his computer and doing publicity for various programs of the church. His forays into the written word were taking him away from contacts with the people. The student's supervisor and Teaching Church Committee members[5] agreed before the meeting to speak honestly with the student about their concerns about him as a future pastoral leader. As the conversation developed and moved toward the end point of the evening, I asked the student why he had come to seminary in the first place. In the quiet moments that followed I believe he came to reframe his self-image: he told the group that his father had been a minister. One day, a few years before the student came to seminary, his father left his church to walk across the street to the local deli for lunch. On his way across the street, which he had crossed hundreds of times, he was hit by a truck and killed instantly. Of course the student knew that he was mourning the loss of his father with whom he had been close. What he did not realize until those quiet moments at the evaluation session was that he had come to seminary to continue to be close to his father and to thereby avoid the full force of his grief. Though this was not part of his conscious decision to enter seminary, it was the driving force behind his decision.

In a recent conversation with students at Drew Theological School, Bishop Neil Irons of The United Methodist Church said that an alarmingly high number of persons in the ministry today are wounded and in need of healing. To an unhealthy degree they need and expect their parishioners to provide the kind of loving acceptance they did not get elsewhere.

His observation matched one of my own, namely that a large number of students come to seminary from troubled backgrounds of one kind or another. In conversations with students about their families of origin, I have been told stories of physical and emotional abuse; sexual abuse by parents, siblings, and extended family members; and unresolved grief from earlier losses. Some students are quite candid about being drawn to the church because it was the one place where they received unconditional love and felt valued in their own right. While I celebrate the healing effect such outreach on the part of the church has for these individuals, I believe that some students come to seminary confusing the love they have found in the church with a call to the ordained ministry. The one does not necessarily follow from the other.

Some students come to seminary, it seems, because they want to be taken care of; they want (and need) to an unhealthy degree the respect, the authority, and the power afforded clergy. Such people are candidates for the codependent relationships that cripple effective ministry by preventing the pastor from offering genuine prophetic and pastoral leadership in the church.

I have known some students over the years who came to seminary because they wanted to explore deeper faith issues and better understand the relationship of faith to life in contemporary society. I once talked with a student who was ready to begin supervised ministry. This young woman had come to Drew three months after finishing college and was bright, enthusiastic, and eager to learn. As we talked about the kind of church that would be the appropriate placement for her, I asked her to tell me what her reasons were for coming to seminary. She said that she wanted to be in a church that was as theologically diverse as possible. I asked her what she hoped to gain from such an experience. After a lengthy silence she said that she was seeking certainty about her own faith. When we talked further about her life prior to coming to seminary, I discovered that she had become a Christian only two years before coming to Drew. Her family had never been churchgoing, and it was only while in college that she had felt drawn to God and the church. She had no real desire to be ordained, but did expect that her faith would become clearer and at the same time strengthened through attending seminary.

After she left my office, I continued to think about her placement in supervised ministry for the next year. I concluded that, instead of the usual supervised ministry experience in which she would try on the role of pastoral leader under close supervision, she needed a type of confirmation experience in which she would be assisted to wrestle with issues of faith as she would have done years earlier had she been in the church at the time.

As these examples show, people come to seminary for highly individualized reasons, which are both conscious and unconscious. Regardless of your reasons for coming to seminary, the decision to enter a program of theological education is an important one with life-changing implications. I hope that you will look at yourself objectively as you read this chapter and allow yourself to think more carefully about the reasons you have come. It is of paramount importance for you to know yourself well if you want to become an effective and helpful pastoral leader. Without such intimate knowledge of yourself, you will not be able to sustain the kind of relationships with others in ministry across the years that are the bedrock of the church. This kind of introspection and self-awareness is at the heart of ministry and will be required of you as you meet your denominational review committee if you choose to pursue ordination.

The sacrifices students make in order to come to seminary, coupled with the conscious and unconscious reasons they come, can serve to create an atmosphere in which expectations of an assured outcome are high. While not every student who has decided to enroll in a theological school is intent upon being ordained upon graduation, many students are. In most Protestant theological schools the Master of Divinity is the primary degree offered; hence, the majority of students are on the path to ordination.[6] The convictions they bring about themselves and the church often serve to shape their ideas about the timeline for their ordination and foreclose their wondering about the rightness of their vocational choice.

The decision to come to seminary is viewed by some students as the end point of a journey to vocational fulfillment. Because of the strength of their conviction about the rightness of this step for their lives, they assume that upon completion of the degree they will be ordained. Some students are confused about the role of the seminary in ordaining people for pastoral leadership. While there is usually a collegial working relationship between theological schools and the denominations they represent, theological schools (unless they are Jewish theological schools) do not ordain people. It is their role to assist students to think critically about issues of ministry within the Christian tradition and the contemporary world. Although such work is obviously relevant to the work of the ordained pastor, it is not a substitute for a thorough process of review administered by the appropriate church body. Each denomination reserves the right to determine whether a given candidate is suitable to be ordained and exercise pastoral leadership within that part of the Body of Christ. Put simply, just because you have come to seminary and are a Master of Divinity student does not mean that you will one day be ordained.

A review of the mainline denominations' ordination processes will make clear the amount of scrutiny involved in review bodies' decisions about candidate's readiness for ordination. Before I turn to that material, however, I want to lay the theological groundwork supporting that scrutiny. I turn now to the father of the Reformation, Martin Luther.

LUTHER: FAITH, VOCATION, AND THE PRIESTHOOD

When Luther nailed the Ninety-five Theses to the church door at Wittenberg in 1519, he was protesting what he judged to be the excesses and abuses of the medieval Catholic Church. Having been a monk himself, he knew firsthand the life of privilege lived in the monastery, which had as its source the growing poverty of the general populace.

In the *Apology of the Augsburg Confession*, Philipp Melanchthon, a reformer and contemporary of Luther, described the monastic life this way:

> Everyone knows how much hypocrisy, ambition, and greed there is in the monasteries; how ignorant and cruel these illiterate men are; and how vain they are in their sermons and in thinking up new ways of making money. There are other vices, too, which we would rather not talk about. Though once upon a time they were schools of Christian instruction, they have degenerated as from a golden age to an iron age, or as the Platonic cube degenerates into bad harmonies which, Plato says, cause destruction. Some of the richest monasteries just feed a lazy crowd that gorges itself on the public alms of the church.[7]

Luther railed against monastic life and all that it represented. He condemned the church hierarchy for its elitist and hierarchical practices along with its theology. Put simply, Luther condemned the belief that it was possible to earn one's salvation and that those in the church hierarchy were superior in some significant way. He argued that the Mass should be in the language of the people, that the Bible belonged to the whole people of God (not just the clergy), and that all were called to ministry by virtue of their baptism. Luther gave many lasting gifts to the church through his courageous stance against Rome. I will highlight three of those gifts here: his understanding of salvation by faith, of vocation, and of the priesthood of all believers.

In contrast with the sale of indulgences and the theology of salvation by works put forward by Catholic clergy, Luther maintained that it was by faith alone that we are saved.

> He, therefore, who does not wish to go astray with those blind men, must look beyond works, and laws and doctrines about works; nay, turning his eyes from works, he must look upon the person and ask how that is justified. For the person is justified and saved not by works nor by laws, but by the Word of God, that is, by the promise of His grace, and by faith, that the glory may remain God's, Who saved us not by works of righteousness which we have done, but according to His mercy by the word of His grace, when we believed.[8]

Any good works done by the believer were the fruits of ordinary Christian living and not the admission ticket into the kingdom of God. Such fruits were to be seen all around wherever believers walked closely with God through Christ and were not limited to those in the church hierarchy. He says of the true Christian,

> He should have no other thought than what is needful for others. That would mean a true Christian life, and that is the way in which faith proceeds to work with joy and love.[9]

As the above quotation notes, the driving force of the Christian's life is the concern for the neighbor that is the result of the indwelling of the Holy Spirit. Luther understood God to be the beneficent provider who knew what his children needed. It was this belief in God's desire to see us provided for that gave rise to Luther's understanding of vocation.

"Vocation" comes from the Latin *vocare*, which means "to call." The word "vocation" can be rightfully understood in different ways. Webster defines it thus:

1. a call, summons, or impulsion to perform a certain function or enter a certain career, especially a religious one;
2. the function or career toward which one believes himself to be called;
3. any trade, profession, or occupation.[10]

Although in today's society we appreciate both the religious and secular meanings of the word, the church at the time of Luther

understood only members of religious orders and the church hierarchy to have received the gift of vocation. Luther understood it
differently. He saw that all Christians had a calling in life, namely
to live the life of faith in God and love for neighbor in whatever
office or station they held. Vocation properly understood was not
confined to an occupation but also included one's relationships
with others. For example, I am not only a person who does a certain job in the work-a-day world, I am also a wife, mother, sister,
voting citizen, teacher, disciple, volunteer, and more. All of these
things are vocations in Luther's understanding. All hold within
them the summons to faithful living as a Christian and are potentially examples of how work in all stations is conducive to the
good of others. "Co-operation takes place in vocation, which
belongs on earth, not in heaven; it is pointed toward one's neighbor, not toward God."[11]

Luther saw that the most common and lowly work of society
was equal to the work of the religious orders of the day. He went
so far as to say that such mean labor could have even more value
than the work of the religious. He wrote:

> However numerous, sacred and arduous they (vows of monkery
> and priesthood) may be, these works in God's sight are in no way
> whatever superior to a farmer laboring in the field, or a woman
> looking after her home. Rather all are measured by him by faith
> alone. . . . Indeed it occurs quite frequently that the common work
> of serving man or maid is more acceptable than all fastings and
> other works of monks and priests where faith is lacking.[12]

By virtue of baptismal vows that were common to both clergy
and laity, all were called to ministry in Christ's name. All had
received a "religious vocation" upon baptism to go into the world
and spread the love of God through Christ through all that they
did. In other words, all Christians were priests. Here Luther's
understanding of the priesthood of all believers:

> Therefore, both vocations—the Ministry, and the vocations of secu-
> lar life which serve love to one's neighbour, spring from the same
> source and arise out of the same Gospel. Since the ministries which
> serve faith and those which serve love take their origin in the same
> source, they possess the same dignity and are different aspects of
> the same priesthood.[13]

In Luther's own words:

> As many of us as have been baptized are all priests without dis-
> tinction ... For thus it is written in I Peter ii, "Ye are a chosen gen-
> eration, a royal priesthood, and a priestly kingdom." Therefore we
> are all priests, as many of us as are Christians.[14]

The legacy of Martin Luther lives on today in the mainline
Protestant denominations. All of these churches presume that
through baptism we are called to service in the world and that God
enables us to be in service through the gifts and graces we have
been given. The question to be asked, therefore, is not "Am I called
to ministry?" but, instead, "To *what kind* of ministry am I being
called?" Behind this latter question lie the distinctions made
between lay and clergy ministry in denominational literature.

DENOMINATIONAL PERSPECTIVES ON MINISTRY AND ORDINATION

Each denomination distinguishes between the ministry of all of
the people of God and the representative ministry of the clergy. For
example, in the Presbyterian Church (USA) *Book of Order* we read:

> All ministry in the church is a gift from Jesus Christ. Members and
> officers alike serve mutually under the mandate of Christ who is
> the chief minister of all.... One responsibility of membership in
> the church is the election of officers who are ordained to fulfill par-
> ticular functions. The existence of these offices in no way dimin-
> ishes the importance of the commitment of all members to the
> total ministry of the church. These ordained officers differ from
> other members in function only.... When women and men, by
> God's providence and gracious gifts, are called by the church to
> undertake particular forms of ministry, the church shall help them
> to interpret their call and to be sensitive to the judgments and
> needs of others.[15]

The Book of Discipline of The United Methodist Church, which is the
"book of law" for that denomination, has a similar statement:

> Ministry in the Christian church is derived from the ministry of

Christ, who calls all persons to receive God's gift of salvation and follow in the way of love and service. The whole church receives and accepts this call, and all Christians participate in this continuing ministry. Within the church community, there are persons whose gifts, evidence of God's grace, and promise of future usefulness are affirmed by the community, and who respond to God's call by offering themselves in leadership as ordained ministers.[16]

In the candidacy manual for the Evangelical Lutheran Church in America we read the following:

It is by Christ's gift that all baptized persons are called to ministry. Every baptized believer is given gifts and abilities for ministry. Every baptized believer is called to ministry in daily life. Some are given gifts and abilities which equip them to provide leadership in one of the rostered ministries of this church.[17]

A closer look at denominational literature shows that each of the mainline traditions has a review process that is designed to help the church discern which type of ministry best suits its candidates. In addition, each denomination assumes that the gifts necessary for ordained ministry will be readily apparent to the church. Consequently, candidates desiring to be ordained must be supported by their home church in which their membership has resided for a minimum of six months.[18] The assumption behind 0ordained ministry is hearing correctly. It is the work of the church to help persons refine their understanding of God's call and to discriminate between those who are suitable for ordained ministry and those who are not. Once again, the assumption is that not everyone sensing a call to ordained ministry should be ordained. Discernment about the call is implicit in each ordination process.

The Presbyterian Church (USA) has a process divided into inquiry and candidacy phases. You will notice that the language describing both phases is one of discernment about the rightness of the pursuit of ordination for this candidate.

The purpose of the inquiry phase is to provide an opportunity for the church and for those who believe themselves called to ministry of the Word and Sacrament to explore that call together in such a way that a decision regarding the inquirer's suitability for ministry of the Word and Sacrament will be based on knowledge and experience of one another. . . . The purpose of the candidacy phase is to provide for the full preparation of persons to serve the church as ministers of the Word and Sacrament. This shall be accomplished through the guidance and evaluation of candidates, using learning contracts within a context of supportive relationships.[19]

That ordination is not guaranteed even upon becoming a candidate is obvious from G-14.0312:

An inquirer or candidate may, after consultation with the session and the committee on preparation for ministry, withdraw from covenant relationship. . . . A presbytery may also, for sufficient reasons, remove an individual's name from the roll of inquirers or candidates, reporting this action and the reasons to the session, to the individual, and, if appropriate, to the educational institution in which the individual is enrolled.

The ordination process in The United Methodist Church involves a series of interviews over a period of time. The candidate meets with and is evaluated by the local congregation in which the candidate's membership resides, a district committee on ordained ministry, and the annual conference board of ordained ministry. A careful reading of the following paragraphs shows that, like the Presbyterian Church (USA), The United Methodist Church does not assume that the candidate's desire to be ordained is the decisive factor. The Church reserves the right to discriminate between candidates all along the ordination process.

The historic questions asked of all candidates for ministry in The United Methodist Church and containing John Wesley's standards for pastoral leaders are found in the *Discipline*. The church has used these questions since they were first asked by John Wesley at the third conference of Methodist preachers in 1746. The questions indicate that the ordination process is one of discrimination and discernment on the part of the church as well as the candidate. Referring to the candidate Wesley asked:

1. Do they know God as pardoning God? Have they the love of God abiding in them? Do they desire nothing but God? Are they holy in all manner of conversation?

2. Have they gifts, as well as evidence of God's grace, for the work? Have they a clear, sound understanding; a right judgment in the things of God; a just conception of salvation by faith? Do they speak justly, readily, clearly?
3. Have they fruit? Have any been truly convinced of sin and converted to God, and are believers edified by their service?

As long as these marks concur in them, we believe they are called of God to service. These we receive as sufficient proof that they are moved by the Holy Spirit.[20]

These questions assume a level of commitment and spiritual maturity in persons seeking ordination. Implicit within them is the expectation that not all persons will be found suitable for ordained ministry. Those who are suitable will become obvious to the church, which reserves the right to examine candidates:

> Those whom the Church ordains shall be conscious of God's call to ordained ministry, and their call shall be acknowledged and authenticated by the Church. God's call has many manifestations, and the Church cannot structure a single test of authenticity. Nevertheless, the experience of the Church and the needs of its ministry require certain qualities of faith, life, and practice from those who seek ordination.[21]

At the beginning of the process, then, this message is given: just because you believe you are being called to ordained pastoral leadership in The United Methodist Church does not mean that your sense of call will be ratified by the church.

One final example is found in the Evangelical Lutheran Church's *Candidacy Manual*. The work of the Candidacy Committee is described thusly:

> Candidacy Committees have the responsibility to determine which form of ministry is most appropriate for the individual's gifts and abilities. When an individual's gifts are not suited for rostered ministry it is the responsibility of the committee to clearly indicate that and direct the individual to the important ministry of the baptized. When an individual does possess those characteristics which enable a person to serve in rostered ministry the committee will need to affirm and support the candidate in the process of preparation and formation.[22]

These examples all point out the reality facing those who have their hearts set upon being ordained upon finishing seminary: the call you feel must be ratified by the church or you will not be ordained. It is not sufficient for you to love God and the church, for you to have been an active church person prior to entering seminary, or for you to graduate from theological school with honors. You may have all of those things and still not be ordained. You may be told that while you clearly have gifts for ministry, you do not appear to have the gifts and evidence of God's grace necessary for *ordained* leadership in the church.

I want to emphasize leadership gifts, not the act of ord.

STUDENTS' EXPECTATIONS OF THEOLOGICAL EDUCATION

Having looked at the ordination process, we turn again to theological education. In addition to the previously noted conscious and unconscious reasons people come to seminary, students come with multiple expectations about what their seminary experience will be like.

I began seminary three months after I graduated from college at the age of twenty-one. The night before I left for seminary, I was at once excited and frightened about what lay ahead of me. I had wanted to be ordained since I felt called to ministry at the age of thirteen. Although I had enjoyed my college years immensely, I was always aware that they were only a means to an end: I wanted to be ordained. My excitement in going to seminary lay in the reality that in seminary I was several steps closer to my goal. Further, I had been challenged and invigorated by my study of the Bible and philosophy in college and was eager to continue to study in these areas. Finally, I expected that I would enter a community that would welcome me and share my enthusiasm for Christianity and ministry in the contemporary world. I expected my seminary experience to confirm my already firm faith, round out my knowledge in necessary ways, and prepare me for almost any situation in ministry. I did not know it then, of course, but I was about to embark on a difficult, and at times, exhausting journey. I also did not know at the time that I had come to seminary with a set of flawed expectations. I expected to be prepared for all eventualities in ministry through the experience. That was my goal. I did not realize that goal was an inappropriate one at the time and was confused when I was frustrated by the experience.

Many students come with similar expectations: they view seminary as the place where they will learn the "how to's" of ministry; a place where they will find their faith deepening automatically; a time when they will be confirmed and affirmed in their desireto be ordained. Perhaps you have come with similar expectations.

The problem with these expectations is that they contain a view of theological education that is flawed in multiple, serious ways. They suggest that seminary is a place with enough and definitive answers to specific as well as universal questions and that it is possible to prepare people to face *any and every* situation in life and ministry.

This view of seminary is flawed both in its anthropology, and its theology. It views humanity as static, and civilization as unchanging. I can only expect to arrive at a state of preparedness for all situations if things never change and tomorrow is predictably like yesterday. If that were the case, I would be able to learn a series of responses to the limited situations that will arise in the future. Such a view is based upon an anthropology that says that you and I are not influenced by the world around us in new ways every day, that there is nothing new under the sun. The issues facing the church today, it follows, are the same issues that have faced the church since Pentecost. Were this view true, the people in the church would think the same predictable thoughts, feel the same feelings, and conclude the same things as did their forebears in the faith. Any student of humanity knows, however, that this view is not reality.

This anthropology is also, of course, theologically flawed. It says that it *is* possible for us to know all we need to know once and forever, and it thereby forgets the lesson of the Garden of Eden: that God alone is omniscient. Further, it denies the truth of the church's doctrine of sanctification: namely that the life of the Christian lived closely with God is one in which it is possible to become more Christlike through use of the spiritual disciplines. In other words, it denies what Peter and Paul knew to be the truth, namely, that the encounter with Christ causes one to change.

You may think at this point that my critique of students' expectations is itself flawed. You may say in response something like the following: "Well, of course, I *know* I can't be prepared for everything that will come my way." I don't doubt that you know that reality on some level. And yet, I have heard many students (and seasoned clergy) complain about the inadequacy of their theological education in preparing them for ministry. The assumptions behind these complaints are that the seminary could have and should have done a better job preparing them for ministry. The charge against the seminary, then, is dereliction of duty. I have also heard judicatory officials wonder about the kind of candidates presenting themselves for ordination today and imply that the seminary did not "do its job" because the candidates are inadequate in some significant way. This complaint implies that the seminary could have done more than it did to prepare candidates for the realities of church life and leadership today.

While no curriculum is perfect, these complaints would only serve as a legitimate critique of theological education if it were possible to prepare students for every situation that will arise. In a world that changes quickly, is complex and ambiguous, and has technological capability which far outdistances its moral maturity—in our world—it is simply not possible to cover everything or prepare for all that will come your way in ministry.

To critique theological schools on the grounds that they did not prepare you adequately is, therefore, unfair and misses the point. It is neither possible nor theoretically desirable for theological education to prepare you for every occurrence in ministry. Instead it is the job of theological education to teach you how to think critically and theologically about issues of faith and life and ministry. The faculty of your school no doubt view themselves as being able to teach you not so much what to think, but *how* to think. Such critical thinking is of greater value in the long run because it will help you face the issues confronting you with insight and integrity.

I return to the work of Paulo Friere in *Pedagogy of the Oppressed*. Recall his contrast of "bank deposit" education and "problem-posing" education. The former consists of the teacher sharing necessary knowledge with the students who then remember that knowledge to be used during tests. In this kind of education, the students are dependent upon the insights, wisdom, and understanding of the teacher. They are not challenged to think for themselves or to be actors in their own history.

Friere argues for the necessity of pedagogy being instead the "problem-posing" kind, in which the teacher is a co-learner with the students and all are called upon to think critically, utilizing the intellectual and experiential resources available. In this type of education, all parties share the roles of student-teacher. It is this type of pedagogy that is more often the norm in theological education today.

You will be expected to think critically about yourself and for yourself. You will have to assimilate vast amounts of material at the same time that you critique its applicability to your life and ministry. I will say more about all of this in a subsequent chapter. I raise the issue now because I hope you will reframe your expectations about what your time in seminary will be like.

Having spoken about the ordination processes in the church today, and discussed briefly the nature of pedagogy prevalent in theological education, I turn now to metaphors. A common metaphor for theological education for many students is that of arrival. Seminary is seen as the place to which they have been propelled by a variety of things. Because it is so closely linked to the destination of ordination, students view themselves on some level as having arrived when they enter seminary.

Although in a certain sense it is true that coming to seminary seems for many students like a homecoming (especially if they have come after years of thinking about ministry or having left other careers that were unsatisfactory), arrival is a dangerous metaphor. It suggests an end point instead of a beginning, and short circuits the kind of wondering about vocational choice that is a part of the spiritual formation needed in pastoral leaders. Adopting arrival as the predominant metaphor for your seminary experience can lead you to foreclose the kind of spiritual, psychological, and intellectual wrestling that is a necessary part of the formation of pastoral leaders.

THEOLOGICAL EDUCATION: A JOURNEY

A more appropriate tack would be to reframe this view of your seminary experience and adopt instead the metaphor of journey. The metaphor of journey is a beloved one in the Judeo-Christian heritage because it is so very representative of the truth about our lives and our relationship with God. To be alive is to be always changing and growing; to be spiritually alive is to be continually deepening one's relationship with the Transcendent and to God's "good creation" and at the same time to be shaped by these relationships. Both of these statements reflect movement from one place or state of being to another. They also reflect the truth at the heart of the universe, namely that it is in the nature of creation that life is complex, mysterious, and dynamic, not static. That this is so has been evident from the beginning of time, for the Genesis account of creation records the movement from chaos to order, from the void to the garden.

The Judeo-Christian heritage acknowledges Abraham as the father of the faith. It is interesting to note that the history of salvation and covenant relationship with God begins with God's calling Abraham to a journey into the unknown: "Go from your country and your kindred and your father's house to the land that I will show you. I will make of you a great nation" (Genesis 12:1-2a). Abraham is asked to follow God into the future by giving up the familiar, setting out into the unknown, and to do so trusting God to supply his need. Because of the nature of Abraham's call into the unknown, he is a good model for seminary students who are also being called away from the familiar and into the unknown.

The story of the Exodus marks the salvation of the Jews from the tyranny of Pharaoh. You may find yourself identifying with the Jews in some ways as you learn about their journey from oppressive security, through forty desert years, into the promised land because you have left a life that must have been unsatisfactory in some ways in order to journey on to a better life. Throughout the difficult journey through the desert, the Israelites experienced God as the One with them: "My presence will go with you, and I will give you rest" (Exodus 33:14).

After the Exodus accounts, the spirituality of journey that is so evident in the Old Testament is best exemplified in the Psalter. The book of Psalms is, in its essence, a love story about the people of Israel and their God. Full of their everyday struggles as sometimes faithful, sometimes unfaithful people, the Psalms contain the whole human drama of misery and redemption. If you have not already studied the Psalms, I hope you will do so while you are in seminary. They contain every known emotion, are wonderfully earthy and passionate, and resound with hope in God and humankind. It is their unqualified honesty and their raw candor with God that makes them my own favorite part of scripture. They contain the journey of the Israelites from faith to greater faith. They express the fears and hopes, the despair and salvation of the psalmists and the conviction that wherever they are on this spiritual journey, God is with them. "Where can I go from your spirit? Or where can I flee from your presence? If I ascend to heaven, you are there; if I make my bed in Sheol, you are there" (Psalm 139:7-8).

In the New Testament, the theologies of journey are central in the interpretation of God's saving work in Christ. Following his baptism in the river Jordan (Matthew 3:13-17), Jesus is led by the Spirit into the desert to share the wilderness and temptation experiences of his people. The forty days Jesus spends there parallel the forty years of the Israelites in the desert in that the spiritual journey contained in both is one of testing and desolation. Jesus is victorious as he is resolutely faithful to God, and he is able to begin his public ministry following his time of testing.

Continuing the metaphor of spiritual journey, we see that Jesus' life was a journey from Galilee to Jerusalem. His public ministry was one in which he moved from place to place proclaiming the kingdom of God. In Luke 9:58 we read about his nomadic existence: "Foxes have holes, and birds of the air have nests; but the Son of Man has nowhere to lay his head." His movement from place to place, unencumbered by mortgages or rent, both fostered and expressed his utter reliance upon God for his material needs and thereby served to daily deepen his intimacy with God.

When he finally journeyed up to Jerusalem and faced the inevitable horrible end to his earthly life, he chose a course from which he would not stray. In the agonizing struggle in the garden of Gethsemane, the triumph of his spiritual journey was revealed when he prayed finally, "Yet, not my will but yours be done" (Luke 22:42). His acceptance of and preference for God's will over his own was the apex of his spiritual journey. He died to himself and was indeed one with God.

We have seen how the people of God have used the metaphor of journey to express the reality of their walk with God since the beginning of covenant history. This simple metaphor, so common in our experience of secular life, is eminently useful for theological school students with the twin goals of faith formation and preparation for lifelong service in ministry. Your time in seminary should be a time of soul searching and exploration, of wondering about yourself and about God, and of pursuit of meaning in life related to vocational choice. Properly understood, it is a time of discernment in which you discover with greater clarity the exact nature of ministry to which you are being called.

I have often asked students beginning their supervised ministry requirement to suspend for the time being any convictions they may have about their belonging in the role of pastoral leader. Instead I urge them to use their experience in the church under supervision to test their call and to wonder with each act of ministry about the "fit" between them and the ministry in which they are engaged. This suspension of their convictions about their call allows them to be more open to feedback and evaluation from others. It also helps them to become more attuned to the still small voice within that can guide them to firmer and more appropriate decisions about vocational direction in the future.

I urge you to do the same as you move through this book and your degree program. Understand yourself as being on a journey with God in which you will discover who you are and where God is leading you. Know that with God's help you will gain clarity about the nature of ministry to which you are being called: ordained or lay. Allow yourself to lean on God and your community and receive from both the encouragement and insight about yourself that you will need to make important decisions about your life.

What are your expectations of sem. & have they been impacted by this reading?

EXERCISE

Think about the issues raised in this chapter in relation to yourself, and if possible, discuss them with someone else. What is it you seek that you expect to find in seminary? When did you first think about going to seminary? When did you first begin to think you were called to ministry? What situations and events brought you to consider ministry as your own vocational choice?

What do you think God wants you to do with your life? How is a theological education relevant and necessary for you to live out what you understand to be God's claim upon your life?

Given that people come to seminary for a variety of healthy and/or unhealthy reasons, look deeply within yourself and make a list of the reasons you now think you have come. As you review that list, does it confirm your decision to come or make you question that decision?

Prayer: Most Gracious and Loving God, you have blessed me all my life—bless me now as well. You have brought me safely to this place, this point in time; continue to walk with me. You have called me to ministry, given me gifts to share with others, graced my life in countless ways, and I am grateful. I do not know how the ministry you are calling me to will unfold. I do not know where I will serve, or how, or with whom. I am uncertain about my readiness and sometimes wonder whether the life of service is really for me. Are you really calling me to some kind of ministry in this broken and hurting world? You told the disciples to simply follow you. Surely you know that it is not always that simple. Sometimes the road is steep and difficult; sometimes visibility is limited and poor. And sometimes the sun shines and the wind is a gentle breeze at my back. At all times, my Beloved Friend, walk with me. Draw me close to yourself as a mother hen draws her chicks under her wings. There I will be protected; there I will be safe. In your loving care it will not matter whether I know the exact details of your summons to service. I will rest peacefully in the certain knowledge that as you have called me, so you will continue to walk with me. That assurance is all I ever really need, Precious Savior. In the name of all that is Holy, I pray. Amen.

CHAPTER 4

Life Together: Variety and Community

Are all apostles? Are all prophets? Are all teachers? Do all work miracles? 1 Corinthians 12:29

A butcher, a baker, a candlestick maker . . .
from "Three Men in a Tub," nursery rhyme

n the United Methodist ordination process, candidates are asked the following question found in the *Discipline* (¶ 321.4*b*):

Are you willing to relate yourself in ministry to all persons without regard to race, color, national origin, social status, or disabilities?

The question clearly expects that candidates should be prepared to enter into relationships with all kinds of people from all kinds of backgrounds. The United Methodist Church is diverse by design; any member of the clergy in the church must be likewise committed to working with and relating to diverse groups of people.

Most mainline denominations today embrace the spirit of that ordination question. They expect their clergy to be willing and comfortable working toward the elimination of the walls separating the different ethnic groups in this country and to be beyond the racism that continues to plague many of our institutions.

Many seminaries offer students exposure to diverse populations of people who have come to study theology and its related disciplines. In this chapter I will discuss the multiple ways diversity is present in many seminary communities. Such diversity provides you with the opportunity to learn about yourself and about others quite different from you. It also gives you the chance to form meaningful relationships with people who may view life quite differently. Such experiences can be life-changing ones that will not only enrich your life while you are in seminary but also enrich your future ministry.

As the apostle Paul knew, God has showered humankind with a splendid variety of gifts and talents, all of which are necessary for the ultimate well-being of the world. In 1 Corinthians 12, Paul has given us one of the most beautiful metaphors for the church, the Body of Christ.

> For just as the body is one and has many members, and all the members of the body, though many, are one body, so it is with Christ. For in the one Spirit we were all baptized into one body—Jews or Greeks, slaves or free—and all were made to drink of one Spirit. . . . Now you are the body of Christ and individually members of it. (1 Corinthians 12:12-13, 27)

In his desire to explain the unexplainable, he chose the image that was familiar to everyone. The people at Corinth had eyes and ears and feet, and could appreciate the interconnection of these organs. As they knew, each of these parts is essential to the whole, yet distinct and special in its own right.

Likewise in the church, Paul went on, there are various gifts given and jobs to be done. All gifts are given for the good of the whole Body, and all jobs are essential for the whole to thrive. There is no room for boasting about one's gifts, nor is there any space for arrogance about one's position or job in the community. All are of equal importance.

Paul was not the last person to observe the variety of talents given humankind. Martin Luther understood all baptized Christians as having vocations that contributed to the general welfare of humankind. All jobs were of equal importance to the world, all work sacred work because of that. The nursery rhyme also notes the different jobs needed to make society run smoothly: A butcher, a baker, and a candlestick maker all contribute important yet quite different gifts to the well-being of their community.

A similar variety of talents and vocations is seen in theological education today. Because Paul reminds us that God showers us with multiple gifts, it should come as no surprise that we see a similarly splendid array of gifts and talents as seminaries admit more and more second- and third-career people. I have been privileged to know students from all walks of life who have come to Drew seeking more meaning in their lives, ready to leave behind careers that once held meaning and joy for them. The list that follows is representative of the variety of work that seminary students have done prior to entering a theological degree program.

Students have come to Drew from these backgrounds and more: professional writer/editor; medical doctor; chiropractor; psychotherapist; landscape architecture; homemaker; nurse; teacher; insurance adjuster; corporate executive; human resources director; lawyer; police officer; all branches of the military; day care center owner/director; banker; hotel and restaurant manager; television producer; news anchor; radio announcer; actor; artist; farmer; local pastor; accountant; museum curator; social worker; nursing home administrator; alcoholism counselor; college engineering professor; business owner; computer programmer; stockbroker; circus worker.

As you can see, people from all walks of life feel called to ministry. This is no doubt the case in the seminary that you are attending. Such a varied background of experiences enriches classroom discussions immeasurably and contributes as well to community life. People who have owned their own homes and businesses; who have held very responsible and creative positions; who have raised families; and who have been married, widowed, or divorced, as well as people who are single, all come together in seminary and bring their past experiences and interests with them. Students who come to seminary right out of college also have an impressive list of interests and accomplishments, including backgrounds in athletics, drama, science, study abroad, literature, and so forth.

In chapter three I noted the age range of people coming to seminary today and briefly discussed some of the healthy and unhealthy reasons people decide to pursue ordination. In this chapter, I explore in more detail multiple levels of influence such varied backgrounds have upon community life. I also discuss the impact such variety can have upon individuals and the relationship of community life to ministry. I invite you to look at the seminary community of which you are a part as comprising the following elements: the students, faculty, and staff—along with their experiences, challenges, dreams, sorrows, disappointments, successes, failures, hopes, and faith commitments. It is as if all of these elements are swirling around the community, shaping and changing it with the arrival of each new idea and day.

I turn now to a deeper discussion about the variety of professional experience and interests represented in Protestant seminaries today. As I said above, this list of professions present in Drew Theological School over the past sixteen years is not exhaustive, merely representative. If it is true that we are drawn to our occupations because they meet some deep need within us that speaks to our history and personality, then a quick reading of the list above makes evident the many different types of persons entering seminary today. From math teachers and accountants and police and military personnel, who presumably appreciate order and precise answers, to artists and actors and circus workers, who are drawn to beauty and excitement, to farmers and gym teachers and landscape architects, who appreciate the world of nature and physical activity we see that within a single seminary community there is likely to be a wide variety not only of interests but of ways of thinking and articulating ideas and faith.

A philosophy of religion class, for example, may be quite interesting and exciting for an actor or artist who is used to thinking expansively and lives comfortably with ambiguity. The same class may be more challenging for a former math teacher or engineer who is used to living in a more precise, ordered world. Likewise a preaching class may be the favorite for those students who have had experience with public speaking (former teachers or actors), but it may be the most difficult class for those who have had little or no time in the spotlight (homemakers or farmers).

Lest you begin to worry about the contributions your background will make to your seminary experience, I urge you to put all worry aside and instead celebrate all that you bring to the community. In speaking with the man who came to Drew after having been a landscape architect, I discovered that he was afraid that he had nothing to draw upon from his former life that would assist him either in seminary or in ministry. After all, what could days spent designing landscapes that would enhance the beauty of their surroundings and move the people who viewed them to appreciate the display of nature in front of them possibly contribute to future days spent with people struggling to make sense of the world and their place in it?

I challenged the man to resist the obvious temptation to check his prior work and experience at the door of Seminary Hall. Instead I invited him to think about the creativity needed in his former work, his attention to detail that had to have been a part of it, the use of his imagination that enabled him to envision a better way of being in a particular space, and the ability to transform that vision into a reality. In all of these facets of his work I saw traits that would apply to ministry. He was an administrator, a pragmatic and objective realist, and a dreamer, all at the same time. All of those skills are necessary in ministry today.

I challenge you to do the same kind of thinking about yourself. What did you do before coming to seminary? Did you come just after finishing college? If so, what were your interests in college both in terms of your course work and your extracurricular activities? What do the choices you made while in college tell you about yourself and your interests, your thought patterns, and your approach to life in general? How might those choices, along with your choices about your avocation interests or part-time work, be carried forward to shape your experience in seminary and your ministry in the future?

If you have come to seminary some years after graduating from college, take a look at how you have spent your time since then. If you have been a homemaker, how might your experience of administering a home and providing direction and support for your family contribute to your ability to organize your time in seminary and administer a church in the future? If you have left a career in some other field to come to study for the ministry, think about how that career choice was reflective of who you are (or were at the time of your choice) and can be related to the practice of ministry. Were you an engineer? Think about how your attention to detail and the use of your imagination in creating new structures or systems might apply to exercising leadership through envisioning new ways of outreach in the church. Were you a teacher? How might the principles of education that informed your teaching be transferred to the teaching role of the pastor? Were you in some segment of the media? What insights did you gain about people and persuasion that will help you be a good preacher? Were you a circus worker? What did you learn about excitement and fun and the child within all of us that will help you to design more creative and interesting worship services?

I hope these examples serve as a source of encouragement for you as you think about your life before seminary. I have not yet met the person who was required to leave every shred of the former life behind in order to be a successful seminary student.

That is not to say that all professions lend themselves nicely to the kind of thinking and soul searching necessary in preparing oneself for ministry. Some lifestyles and work lend themselves more easily to being in seminary and ministry than others. For example, social workers and psychotherapists seem to have a fairly easy time translating their prior work and study to the theological fields.

On the other hand, I have spent a great deal of time with students that have come to seminary after having been police officers or military personnel. I feel a particular kinship with these students and their families since my husband has been in law enforcement for the past twenty-two years. Because of his work and our life together, I have been able to see firsthand the particular challenges facing people who move from those positions into ministry.

In order to be a successful police officer or member of the military, a person must cultivate the ability to be detached from the emotional side of life to a greater degree than does the general population. Vulnerability is often a detriment in these fields; life within the system is ordered and predictable; and suspicion is rewarded. (As my husband has often told me, he is "paid to be suspicious!") Ministry almost always calls for another way of being in the world. Pastors must be well acquainted with their own feelings, able to express them appropriately and assist others to do the same, allow themselves to be vulnerable to the pain of others, and assume the best instead of the worst. As any seasoned pastor can tell you, ministry is far from being always neatly ordered, and the only predictable thing about it is that each day is different and the life of the pastor is highly unpredictable!

Patterns of living prior to coming to seminary will make it easier or more difficult to adjust to the world of theological education and life in the church. Failure to take seriously the relationship of prior work and life experience to ministry will put future ministry at risk.

You may find that you have mixed feelings about being in seminary, especially if you have left work that was at one time very satisfying. It may be that you left it because it was only partially satisfying at the end; it may be that you were forced to leave because of "downsizing";[1] it may be that you left because you had deferred your dream of service long enough. Whatever your reasons, be aware that you may have some grief work to do in order to genuinely leave that former life behind. That you have grief work to do does not necessarily mean that you should not be in seminary. It simply may mean that there were parts of your former work that you genuinely liked and that you miss them while at the same time you recognize the rightness of your decision to move on. In other words, you may be ambivalent about the changes in your life. Not only is that to be expected, your ambivalence can be a valuable introduction to the complexities that you will need to address in multiple ways before you are ready to be an effective pastor.

Whatever your background has been, you need to take a critical look at yourself in order to begin to think objectively about yourself in ministry as was discussed in the second chapter. Some seminaries have required discussion groups for entering students in which they explore these identity issues in detail over the first semester or year. Other seminaries do not have such groups. Whether your seminary facilitates this kind of self-exploration or not, I hope you will make it a priority for your time of preparation. Community life events, late-night dorm discussions, and intentional small groups run by students all provide arenas for your thinking about these issues.

LIFE CYCLE DEVELOPMENT THEORY AND THE SEMINARY COMMUNITY

A second important factor affecting community life in theological schools is related to the age of the students. Currently there is a wide age range of students in seminary, from college age to retirement age. As we have learned through the work of Erik Erikson, Daniel Levinson, Carol Gilligan, Jean Baker Miller, and others, there is an oscillating rhythm to life as one ages and matures, which presents the individual with opportunities and challenges that bring success and failures. How one moves through these opportunities and challenges determines one's readiness to take on the increasing demands of maturity, intimacy, and productivity in one's life.

This developmental perspective on the life cycle is not a foreign one to students of scripture; the notion of seasons is well developed in scripture's understanding of creation. Solomon offered a view of life that helps us to see, understand, and perhaps embrace the changes necessary for life to be meaningful and rich when he wrote, "For everything there is a season, and a time for every matter under heaven" (Ecclesiastes 3:1).

Solomon's timeless wisdom about the rhythmic and seasonal nature of life has been substantiated in modern times by discoveries about the psychological and social pathways to mature citizenship. There is wide acceptance today of the notion that humanity matures psychologically, socially, and spiritually over time and as a result of successfully facing and working through fairly predictable challenges and opportunities at predictable ages. Before I turn to the particular constellation of developmental themes present in theological schools with diverse student bodies, I will quickly review the field of developmental psychology.

We are indebted to Sigmund Freud (1856–1939) for the field known broadly as "depth psychology." Freud created a theory of personality that encompassed unconscious as well as conscious aspects, and showed how personality development in later life is an extension of one's childhood development. As Freud discovered, our past is in our present in significant and influential ways.

Freud's colleague, Carl G. Jung (1875–1961), can justly be considered the father of the modern study of adult development. Although for most of Jung's thirties he was closely related to Freud and was a leading member of the newly forming psychoanalytic movement, in 1913 he split from Freud and gradually formed his own school, analytical psychology. Jung's primary interest was in adult psychospiritual development, "the second half of life," and he tried to understand individual development as a function of both internal processes and external cultural forces. He saw that as a part of normal development we progress through emotional involvements and conflicts and that the personality cannot reach its full growth by age 20. Jung found that the next opportunity for fundamental change starts at about 40, "the noon of life," and he used the term "individuation" for the developmental process that begins then and may continue until death.

Perhaps the best-known contemporary figure in developmental psychology is Erik Erikson (1902–1994). Erikson was concerned with the whole of the life span and its challenges at each stage of life. He developed a theory of psychosocial crises from birth to death, highlighting the character trait hidden within either the successful resolution of the crisis or the failure of the same. His pioneering work in the field of developmental psychology showed that the mature, compassionate, responsible adult has moved successfully through several psychosocial crises. To fail to successfully resolve these crises means that development is arrested and future maturation is handicapped. Erikson listed the crises as follows:

Psychosocial Crises in the Life Cycle[2]

Age:	Psychosocial Crisis:
1. Infancy	Trust vs. Mistrust (hope)
birth to 12 or 18 months	(belief in something)
2. Early Childhood	Autonomy vs. Shame and Doubt
1 to 3 years	(will power)
3. Play Age	Initiative vs. Guilt
3 to 5 years	(purpose)
4. School Age	Industry vs. Inferiority
6 to 11 years	(competence)
5. Adolescence	Identity vs. Identity Diffusion
12 to 18 years	(fidelity)
6. Young Adult	Intimacy vs. Isolation (love)
18 to 30 years	
7. Adult	Generativity vs. Stagnation
30 to 60 years	(care)
8. Older Adult	Ego Identity vs. Despair
60 years plus	(wisdom)

Erikson showed through his research that although each one of us is unique in many ways, we are also similar in many important ways.

At least it is the case that we face similar challenges in life, similar tasks and hurdles if we are to progress steadily to the point at which we become contributing and responsible members of society.

Insights from the field of psychology supply us with a map of sorts by which we can think about what it means to be a mature adult and how we get there. They are particularly useful to us as we consider the makeup of theological school student bodies today with the wide range of ages represented in them.

As was noted in chapter three, theological schools today enjoy student bodies made up of men and women from their twenties to their sixties (and sometime beyond!). In 1993–94 29 percent of the men were over 40 years of age. That means that 71 percent of male students were under forty. Similarly, 43 percent of the female students enrolled at that time were over 40 while 47 percent were under.[3]

No doubt you have already noticed that you share some concerns and goals with your generational partners. The purpose of this discussion is to invite you to think developmentally about yourself and your colleagues in community. Imagine the richness of community life when the community is made up of people facing different challenges developmentally. A twenty-two-year-old wondering whether or not she is capable of graduate level study has different fears than the forty-five-year-old businessman who is apprehensive about being able to study as he once did. A sixty-year-old grandfather who wonders how many active years in ministry he will have upon graduation feels the weight of the passage of time in a different way than the woman who is thirty and views the long road between the present and her retirement forty years from now with satisfaction. Students who come to theological school bringing with them a solid belief in themselves, having been nurtured in a secure and stable family, will experience the upheaval attending theological education in different ways than those students who arrive at seminary uncertain about who they are and still needing to develop the capacity for intimacy that is the foundation of ministry.

You will discover that within your community there are different understandings of ministry between male and female students. Not surprisingly given the insights of the developmental psychologists and current understandings of issues of sexuality, women and men tend to emphasize different aspects of pastoral leadership. Women in ministry tend to be relationship oriented while men tend to be more task oriented. Women also tend to spend more time thinking and *worrying* about how to combine ministry with family time so that balance is achieved and family (especially the children) do not suffer from the mother's decision to enter ministry. This is not to say that men are not concerned with family life, for they obviously are. The emphasis placed on it, however, and the public concern expressed about it are different for men than women.

LIFESTYLE AND OTHER DIFFERENCES

There are other ways seminary communities are affected by the circumstances of their members. In your community you will find students who are single, married, divorced, and widowed. Students in each case will bring different issues to address and gifts to share with the community. As you might imagine, each lifestyle has challenges and opportunities within it.

Single students come often to seminary being responsible for themselves only, and they may tend to have fewer demands upon their time.[4] Although they may work in addition to attending school, their nonwork and nonschool hours may be used at their discretion without fear of neglecting spouse or children. More discretionary time may give them more study time, which is certainly desirable. Being single may, however, mean the student is isolated from the outside world. Single students may have difficulty forming intimate relationships with others outside seminary because it is difficult to understand the world of theological education unless one is a part of it and because the weekly schedule of seminary students is so full. I have heard many single students lament the fact that they either have no time to form new and sustaining personal relationships or they are not sure how to go about doing so. Some students (both single and married) have already noticed that friends and family are not sure how to relate to them once their decision to enter the ministry has been announced.

Without the built-in support system of a family, single students can find seminary to be a lonely time of soul searching.

Discussions about forming and maintaining satisfying, intimate relationships while in ministry are common in seminary dorms for good reason. Seminary students, like everyone else, are created to be in relationship. Personal relationships that nurture and sustain single students in seminary are as important and necessary as the marriage relationship is for married students. Relationships formed within the seminary community can help to offset any feelings of isolation from the world beyond seminary, and they can prove instructive about developing future friendships when one is in full-time ministry.

You will also find students whose marriages are secure and stable along with those whose marriages begin to shake under the pressures of one spouse being in school. Put simply, it is difficult to describe the excitement and intensity of being in the crucible of seminary life. Married students must, by definition, take extra care to see that they are involving their spouses as much as possible in their evolving intellectual and spiritual lives. To fail to do so will inevitably mean that the nonstudent spouse feels excluded and unimportant in the new life of the seminarian.

This reality of spouses growing at different rates is common in programs of higher education. It is the most natural thing in the world for married couples to be out of step with each other relative to professional development and to grow apart because of it. Couples in which one spouse is enrolled in seminary are even more at risk for this than those in other schools.

I have known couples who grew a great deal closer while one of them was in seminary. In those cases the nonseminary spouse took great pride in the development of the other spouse, became involved in community life activities whenever possible, and had at the same time a satisfying life lived apart from the seminarian.

I have also known couples whose relationships (some of which were troubled long before they came to seminary) were damaged irreparably by the experience. In those cases, the nonseminary spouse usually did not want to be the spouse of a clergyperson, was not supportive emotionally, felt put upon for being thrust into the breadwinner's role, and made little attempt to become involved in community life.

Couples with children face additional pressures. Relocating to the seminary environs means that some students will need to enroll their children in a new school system, which is stressful for both parent and child. Finding time to continue familiar patterns of mothering or fathering is difficult once one becomes a student again. Special care needs to be taken to see that children do not suffer neglect because of the busy schedule of the parent who is also a student.

Finally, campus housing can contribute to rising tensions within the seminary student. Going from owning a home or renting an apartment to living in a dorm or an on-campus apartment can be stressful. For single students, sharing space after being on one's own can be a frustrating and demoralizing experience however much a close community develops within the dorm. Noise levels in the dorm can be trying.

Married students who have to cram beloved furniture into space a fraction of the size of their former home and double up siblings in available bedrooms can discover that family members soon get on one another's nerves. Students may need to go to the library every night in order to have some quiet time and space. Although academically important, from the perspective of the family this can mean dissatisfied children and spouses who once again feel like they have been left behind.

Racial and Ethnic Diversity in the Seminary

Seminaries today are also more racially and ethnically diverse. According to the Association of Theological Schools, the racial and ethnic makeup of accredited theological schools in 1996 was the following:

white 67%
black 9%
Asian 7%
Hispanic 3%
non-resident alien 8%
Native American < 1%
race unknown 6%

Most Protestant theological schools today have some diversity within their student bodies that enriches the conversations in classrooms, living spaces, and the common life of the school.

This diversity will be displayed in discussions about issues raised in class and in the community. Different ethnic groups have correspondingly different understandings of the role of the church within the community and the role of the clergy within the church. From democratic perspectives, which view the clergy and laity as equally powerful, to more autocratic views, which expect the clergyperson to be more directive and assertive, you can expect the diversity represented in your student body to be evident in discussions about ecclesiology and the nature and function of the ordained ministry.

Discussions about conflict management in the church, for example, may reveal opposing views of the nature and proper response to conflict on the part of the individual and the community. If we understand the term *culture* to mean the customs, values, and patterns of behavior of a given people, we can appreciate the truth of David Augsburger's insight:

> Each culture invites a wide range of habits, personality styles, and behavioral patterns for use in times of calm or in situations of conflict; and each culture also prohibits and seeks to limit the exercise of what it considers undesirable or unacceptable behavior.[6]

Do not be surprised or dismayed if you hear a colleague speak passionately about an appropriate response in a given situation and you find yourself disagreeing vehemently. Allow yourself to view your colleague's opinion as another way of viewing things, a different facet to the diamond of theological education. These examples are not meant to suggest that one way of being and viewing ministry is better than another. On the contrary, they serve only to highlight the rich diversity you are likely to find in conversations with your colleagues about ministry. I view this aspect of theological education as one of the most valuable contributions to your preparation for ministry because by its nature it is teaching the reality that the people of God are at once similar and unique in important and beautiful ways. To fail to understand that is to fail to be ready to minister effectively in a complex and changing world.

If there are international students in your school, you can expect to be with people who have different languages, idioms, and ways of learning and expressing themselves in class. This kind of diversity is both enriching and challenging for faculty and students. We have learned at Drew that all of us in the school are called upon to examine our assumptions about education and pedagogy, hospitality and community. Our international students have pushed us to be more self-conscious about our everyday assumptions about life in the school and in the world. In so doing they have given us a tremendous gift.

The level of challenge they bring to the indigenous population of the school is more than matched by the challenges they face themselves. At Drew, for example, we have a large number of students from Korea. We have discovered over the years that one of the particular challenges facing them when they come to Drew from Korea is adapting to the Western method of education. Steeped in democracy as we are, we expect our students to be able to speak up in class, asking questions of the professor and sharing ideas freely in discussion groups. We also expect that our students will not agree with every idea posed in class or in the readings and that they will eventually disagree openly while stating their own arguments. Such openness is quite opposed to the Eastern way of education, which views such a free exchange of ideas as inappropriate and disrespectful of the professor.

If your seminary has international students and you have never studied with someone from another country before, I hope you will take the opportunity to get to know them and their culture as you share your own culture with them. If you are yourself an international student, I hope you will likewise use your time in this country to expand your understandings of ministry and theology so that your future ministry will be enriched. Clearly all members of a diverse community stand to gain from such diversity.

Theological Diversity

You may discover that you are now part of a community that includes—in addition to differences in the community regarding age, gender, prior career activity, marital status, and racial and ethnic background—representatives of all points along the theological continuum. Some members of the community will count themselves theologically conservative and more comfortable with orthodox understandings of God in Jesus Christ and literal interpretations of scripture. Others will be more comfortable with more liberal understandings of the nature of God and may even express doubts about the divinity of Jesus Christ.

You may place yourself between these two extremes or discover that your theological views change while you are in seminary. Whatever your theological views, do not be surprised to find people in your community who do not share your views. One of the most exciting and challenging parts of being in seminary is the simple act of sitting in class and listening to the views espoused by faculty and fellow students. Often students have difficulty because they feel their own beliefs come under attack as other views are expressed. Some students feel outside the community because their beliefs are shifting or confused.

Diverse Lifestyle

A final area in which you may see diversity has to do with the lifestyle of the students and faculty in the community. Although denominations differ in their response to the question of homosexual persons being ordained, many seminaries have students who are gay and lesbian, in addition to heterosexual students. Depending upon the school, the tradition it represents, and the makeup of the student body and faculty, you may find yourself being called upon to discuss your deepest feelings about issues of sexuality and lifestyle choices. Regardless of your views on the subject, you will likely find yourself engaging the issues at a deeper level than you ever have before. You may find your original position come under attack; you may be misunderstood, supported, or changed. Whatever the outcome, you need to realize that issues of sexuality go to the heart of what it means to be human and that they need to be discussed in the context of theological education.

Diverse Faculty

Thus far we have looked only at the student members of the theological community. A look at the faculty makeup in ATS accredited seminaries reveals further diversity. ATS reports the following breakdown in its faculty in the 1996–1997 academic year:[7]

white 90%
black 5%
Asian 2%
Hispanic 2%
non-resident alien 3%
Native American < 1%
race unknown < 1%

Obviously schools differ in the numbers of nonwhite faculty present. Although schools with all white faculty may be adept at raising and addressing issues of diversity, racism, and sociological analyses, faculties that are themselves racially and ethnically diverse model in a particular way the realities of the social complexion of this country. If you are fortunate enough to be in a school with a multiethnic faculty, you will be exposed to one more source of diversity as the curriculum and bibliographies used in class are reflective of the whole of humankind. Voices raised around these issues both in the faculty and the student body serve to push students beyond the constraints of their parochial views and understandings of the church.

In this chapter we have discussed the complex nature of the theological community. We have looked at the following dimensions of the human experience: (1) occupations prior to coming to seminary and their impact on seminary students; (2) age of students and their corresponding developmental tasks; (3) gender differences in understandings of ministry; (4) challenges facing single and married students; (5) lifestyles and issues of sexuality; and (6) racial and ethnic diversity in faculties and student bodies.

All of these things are likely to be present in graduate professional schools whose student bodies were made up of primarily second career people. Depending upon the members of the community in question, such diversity may contribute to an unparalleled learning environment in the classroom and beyond. For some members of the community, however, particularly in theological schools, such diversity may be experienced as an onslaught and attack on the views and person of the student in the community. Because the stakes are so high existentially speaking, and because it is in the nature of theological education to raise life's biggest and most important questions, you may come to experience seminary in all its diversity and fullness as a crucible experience.

The term *crucible* has three related meanings,[8] which, when taken together, suggest something that by its very nature forces a change in the structure (or nature) of the elements within it. The holding environment of the metal container is strong enough to withstand great heat and fire while maintaining its shape. The seminary community, likewise, is a similar holding environment. Its provides a strong and dependable container that remains intact despite the fiery blasts of confusion, doubt, and disintegration of former ways of thinking and being in the student body.

The use of *crucible* to mean "a severe test [or] hard trial" is the definition most closely related to life in seminary and the one that points to an essential truth about the total experience. As I said in the first chapter of this book, as a seminary student you will be challenged physically, intellectually, emotionally, and spiritually. You will be expected to renegotiate your faith commitments while being infused with new ideas, experiences, and information all of the time. You will spend long hours studying, working, and perhaps commuting. When all of this is coupled with work in churches you may find that you have little personal time to relax with family and friends. At the same time, you will have the opportunity to handle holy things on a regular basis, to give regular and substantial time to the study of the Word of God, and have frequent occasions to worship God through Christ with your brothers and sisters in the seminary community.

Most Protestant seminaries today know complex levels of diversity not present years ago. You are almost certain to find students with whom you share much in common. Your conscious efforts to reach out to others will help lessen any sense of isolation you feel. They will also help you think about your experience in theological terms from the very beginning.

THEOLOGICAL EDUCATION: BABEL OR PENTECOST?

Two stories from scripture offer rich and fitting metaphors for the seminary experience. You may find yourself feeling closer to one expression than the other during your time at seminary or you may find yourself vacillating between the two.

The two stories are the Tower of Babel and the Day of Pentecost. In Genesis 11:1-9 is recorded the story of the Tower of Babel, which serves as the explanation for the multiple languages spoken by the human race. After the flood, the scene was set in Shinar (Babylonia) where wandering nomads found a plain and decided to establish a city and a way of life. Urged by the desire for unity, they began to build a tower by which they would also make a name for themselves.

> Come, let us build ourselves a city, and a tower with its top in the heavens, and let us make a name for ourselves; otherwise we shall be scattered abroad upon the face of the whole earth. (Genesis 11:4)

The arrogance and self-sufficiency of the nomads that brought them to think themselves capable of "making a name" for themselves on their own, instead of through covenant with Yahweh, resulted in Yahweh's taking action once again. The price for their self-assertion and revolt against God was the confusion of their languages so that they could no longer understand each other. That confusion led to their dispersion in language groups over the face of the earth.

The top portion of the tower of Babylon was referred to as *bab-il*, or "gate of God." By means of a pun on the Hebrew verb "to confuse," the tower became known as the "Tower of Babel."[9] The English word "babble" is related to this story. When we talk about someone babbling on and on, we mean they are not making any sense to those listening.

A second story from scripture talks about diverse peoples being together in a time of understanding and community. In the book of Acts we read the story of the birth of the church at Pentecost (Acts 2:1-13). Fifty days after the Resurrection, the disciples were gathered together in one place. Suddenly there was a great rush of wind through the house where they were sitting, and tongues of fire appeared to rest upon each one of them.

All of them were filled with the Holy Spirit and began to speak in other languages, as the Spirit gave them ability. . . . And at this sound the crowd gathered and was bewildered, because each one heard them speaking in the native language of each. (Acts 2:4, 6)

Anyone acquainted at all with the sorrow that comes and covers everything when a loved one dies knows also the confusion that accompanies that sorrow. We do not know what the disciples were doing in that room only one month and three weeks after their beloved Master had been brutally killed. But we can assume that alongside their marveling at the Resurrection were their confusion about the future and wonder about the meaning of life.

Although the details of the day of Pentecost are lost to us, we have Luke's account of the miracle that took place. After the wind swirled through the room and the flames of fire graced each one's head, the disciples began to speak in different languages. At this point their experience is not unlike that of their Babylonian brothers and sisters who were also speaking in strange tongues. The people gathered around (apparently the scene shifts to outside where Jews from every nation of the world were celebrating Pentecost) heard them and were amazed at what they heard.

Although the crowd was representative of every nation under heaven and, therefore, the people present spoke many different languages, they were each able to recognize their own native language in the words of the disciples. It was like a gathering of United Nations delegates without the need of interpreters!

In both the Babel and Pentecost stories, unfamiliar languages were spoken. In both of these stories God was the agent behind those languages. In both of these stories the relationship between God and the people involved determined whether or not the languages were comprehensible, whether or not the people involved understood. In the final analysis, God made the difference between mass confusion and the hearing of one's very own mother tongue even in a strange land. Side by side, these stories remind us that people are free agents in relationship to God. They can choose to walk closely with God, seeking God's direction, counting on God's wisdom and illumination for dealing with life as it comes, or they can choose to act as if they are entirely self-sufficient, needing no help from "above" or anywhere else. The choice is clearly theirs.

Clearly there are different outcomes depending upon one's ultimate choice. In the two stories we have discussed, the world made sense to those for whom God's presence and strength were the context in which they lived. Instead of trying to "make a name" for themselves on their own as did their Babylonian forebears, the disciples were deliberately seeking God's help and direction. They had just chosen the newest apostle and were clearly wanting to go forward in spreading the gospel of Jesus Christ. Instead of free agents, they might be called "freed agents" who understood in profound ways that they needed God in Christ in order to live, and live abundantly.

The relevance of these stories from our ancient past to theological education today is great. They are reminiscent of the multiple voices heard in the theological community as outlined above. You may find yourself at times feeling like you are at the tower in Babylon, not understanding the different voices around you. You may hear ideas and beliefs and feelings and dreams astoundingly different from your own and wonder how, if at all, you are going to fit into this community. You may sometimes wonder if there is a single other person who speaks the same language that you do or fear that, like your ancient brothers and sisters, you will be forced to go wandering off someplace else to find the family to whom you belong in the faith. You may even wonder if anyone else knows God as you do, loves God as you do, lives with God as you do— or if anyone else shares your passion for ministry.

You will also have times when you feel more connected to others than you ever have in your entire life. You will know the joy that comes from sharing a passion for the Word of God and the deep desire and commitment to make the world a better, more just place for all of God's children. In those times you will know the Pentecost experience when all makes sense and the strange voices around you are not so strange after all.

What I have discovered over the years is that the difference between the two experiences for students in seminary is being open to God and the active presence of the Holy Spirit in their lives. When we invite God into the seminary experience, we begin to see and hear more clearly and understand that the same God may speak through different voices.

The Babylonians aspired to something big! They wanted to make a name for themselves for all eternity. That in and of itself is not entirely bad, for each one of us hopes to also leave our mark for the good on the world. The question for you as you continue in seminary is: what is the name you want to make? One's relationship with God is the key. In both stories the people had a relationship with God. The difference is that in the Babel story God was not the focus of the people, the tower was—and confusion resulted. In the Pentecost story, God was the focus and clarity and direction and the birth of the church resulted.

EXERCISE

Spend some time by yourself, and then in the company of others, thinking about the nature of the community you have joined. How diverse is it? What is the age spread in the student body? the faculty? What different racial and ethnic groups are represented?

What different theological perspectives have you found within the community? What is the impact of all of these realities on you? Do you feel as if you have found some kindred spirits, or do you feel as if you are alone? What are you doing to deepen your connection to the seminary community?

Take some time to think about the story of the Tower of Babel and the story of Pentecost. Which story is more representative of your experience in seminary thus far? Why?

What have you done or do you need to do to move from a Babel experience to a Pentecost experience?

Prayer: Most gracious and loving God, out of the rich storehouse of your love you have created each one of your children to be unique in all the universe. As it is your nature to be generous, you have endowed each one of us with gifts and talents, hopes and dreams that are special to us and beautiful in their own right. Help us to be mindful that in variety is the spice of life along with the evidence of your gracious love. Enable us to be children of Pentecost, enlivened by your spirit, able to speak and listen in ways that make sense to us and others. And through it all, be our Guide and our Friend. In Christ's name we pray. Amen.

CHAPTER 5

The Classroom

The fear of the Lord is the beginning of knowledge; fools despise wisdom and instruction. Proverbs 1:7

Do your best to present yourself to God as one approved by him, a worker who has no need to be ashamed, rightly explaining the word of truth. 2 Timothy 2:15

You shall not oppress a resident alien; you know the heart of an alien, for you were aliens in the land of Egypt. Exodus 23:9

If theological education can kill your faith, your faith is not that strong. Professor Ada-Maria Isasi-Diaz

he night before I was to leave for seminary, many years ago, I received a phone call from a dear friend of our family who had known me from the time I was called into the ministry at the age of thirteen. She was calling with her husband to wish me well and send me off with their love and encouragement. Although I was eager to get into ministry and knew that seminary was the route to that end, in truth I was somewhat anxious and thus delighted to hear from them. In general, however, I was looking forward to the experience and happy to be entering a program that I expected would teach me about God and myself and the world in new and exciting ways.

To my surprise, at the beginning of our conversation I burst into tears; despite my good college record, deep down I was not sure that I was up to graduate school. I needed friends like them to tell me what I all of a sudden could not see for myself: that I would succeed as countless others had before me and that by admitting me the school believed the same.

Perhaps you had similar feelings and fears as you filled out the application for your seminary or theological school. Because of the rich diversity in student bodies today, you will find at least one other person in your community who shares important traits with you. Equally, your feelings about being up to graduate work are shared by others in your community. If you are primarily excited and energized by it, you will discover colleagues who share your eagerness and enthusiasm. If you are intimidated by the prospect, take heart, for you too are not alone. Indeed, sometimes the students who feel the most inadequate are the very ones viewed by their peers as being the most capable in class.

Theological education properly done is a rigorous course of study; it requires long hours of study, personal discipline, stamina, and the hard work of thinking and rethinking one's views and beliefs in light of the insights of the academy. Yet theological education is also significantly different from other vocational programs, for it presses students to consider life's biggest questions and to undertake a fairly thorough process of self-examination in light of the gospel. Niebuhr writes:

> The presence in the theological community of the ultimate objects or subjects of study, like its engagement in serving the ultimate purpose of the Church, means that theological students are personally involved in their work to an unusual degree. The study of the determination of personal and human destiny by the mystery of being beyond being, of the tragedy and victory of the son of man, of the life-giving, healing power immanent in personal and social existence, of the parasitic forces of destruction that infest the spiritual as well as the biological organism, of the means of grace and the hope of glory—this cannot be carried on without a personal involvement greater than seems to be demanded by the study of history, nature or literature.[1]

Niebuhr is correct about the degree to which theological students are intimately and personally involved in their studies. Beyond long hours of study and the sheer physical challenge of getting the chapters read and the papers written on time lies the greater intellectual, emotional, spiritual challenge, namely engaging the twin questions Who is God? and Who am I? This exploration of God and self within the learning community is a lengthy and at times arduous one.

How your own seminary experience proceeds relative to the classroom depends in no small part on what your expectations and attitudes are. In this chapter I address the variety of teaching methods, pedagogical assumptions, and fields of study commonly present in theological schools today. I ask you to consider your prior experiences of higher education and what they have contributed to the ways you think about issues and your expectations of your professors in seminary. And I offer the biblical concept of hospitality as a metaphor for being open to the insights of the academy as one matures intellectually and spiritually.

I begin this study, however, by examining the attitude that intellectual development is the enemy of faith and that theological education is a necessary evil to be endured, perhaps, but also to be guarded against.

Over the course of my years in theological education, I have heard too many students say: "I just want to graduate and get my degree so I can be in ministry" or "I just want to graduate with my faith intact." Some well-meaning people in one student's church warned her to be careful in seminary and to "not let them rob you of your faith!" The attitude behind these comments is that theological education will destroy faith and that therefore the educational process is not to be entirely trusted or embraced.

This fear of the impact of theological education is not always present in students. If you listen closely to your colleagues in class you will hear some of them who seem most eager to have their ideas and beliefs about God expanded and enriched by exposure to critical and new ways of thinking. Although they often come with firm faith commitments, they realize the evolutionary nature of their faith, expect it to change by virtue of their education and are not threatened by change. You will hear other students, however, who seem to be resisting new ideas and what are for them new ways of conceiving of God and the church.

ORIGINS OF SPIRITUALITY

As the psalmist reminds us, we are fearfully and wonderfully made in God's image.[2] Our psychological, spiritual, emotional, and cognitive makeup comes with us into the classroom and has a profound impact on our receptivity to new learning. Our relationship with God, in no small measure a result of this makeup (as well as a determinant of it), is at the heart of the matter in the theological school classroom.

We know, for example, that children's early experiences of parenting and childcare shape their dawning consciousness about God and God's world. That children have spiritual lives is abundantly clear to anyone who has ever spent any time with them. They often tend to speak of God in rather matter-of-fact terms, almost viewing God's existence as obvious to all. Dr. Robert Coles's remarkable book *The Spiritual Life of Children* is the culmination of his conversations and observations of children around the world over a thirty year period. The children in his book represent the Christian, Jewish, and Islamic faiths and reveal a picture of God in whose presence they seem to be fearless. That they sometimes on their own and in the face of great adversity endeavor to make sense of their world and relate the Transcendent One to their current struggles is testimony to the young human spirit Coles encountered. As a psychiatrist, Coles is interested in the conjunction between the spiritual and psychological lives of his young subjects. He writes:

> As I go over the interviews I've done with children, I find certain psychological themes recurring. I hear children (on tape) talking about their desires, their ambitions, their hopes, and also their worries, their fears, their moments of deep and terrible despair—all connected in idiosyncratic ways, sometimes, with Biblical stories, or with religiously sanctioned notions of right and wrong, or with rituals such as prayer or meditation. Indeed, the entire range of children's mental life can and does connect with their religious and spiritual thinking. Moral attitudes, including emotions such as shame and guilt, are a major psychological and sometimes psychiatric side of young spirituality. In this regard, the discourse of children rivals that of Christian saints, such as Augustine and Teresa of Avila and St. John of the Cross.[3]

Whatever the connection is that Coles demonstrates to exist between our psychological and spiritual states, it comes to seminary with us and has an impact on our work in the classroom. Albeit simplistically, we can think of theological education as extended time with God. The literal understanding of the word *theology* is "the study of God" from the Greek *theos* (God) and *logos* (study). Our history with God informs our present as we are pushed to study not only God but ourselves in relationship to God.

I was fortunate enough to be raised in a loving home. My parents, brother and sister, and I attended the Methodist church in town and were quite active in it.[4] My father worked long hours at a job he loved and was involved in community service organizations in addition to his work in the church. My mother was a school teacher at a time when married women were expected to remain at home, thereby giving me a model of an independent and intelligent woman who was eager to share the gifts for teaching that God had given her. She was equally committed to her church and was involved in a variety of classes and groups within the church, offering leadership enthusiastically across the years. Together my parents taught me through word and example that my relationship with God was the most important thing in the world and that God was easy to relate to. God was loving, forgiving, full of mercy, intimately interested and involved in my life, knew me better than I would ever know myself, and in control of the world. When I arrived at college and entered the preministerial track, I brought with me a solid relationship with God nurtured across the years by a conservative faith and belief that God was in charge and that one day all would be right with the world (even if now it was not). I understood God (I thought) and felt good about my relationship with the one I called Friend. The backdrop for that relationship was, of course, my relationship with my parents. I had no trouble, for example, referring to God as "Father" because my own father was a loving, forgiving man who left no doubt that his family was a high priority for him. My mother, the other authority in my life, mixed discipline and love in equal and appropriate parts. I respected rather than feared my parents. For the most part, we had an easy style of relating that was fulfilling and reassuring as I made my way in the world of my youth.

How I feel about God, as well as what I think about God, has an impact not only on my present relationship with God but also on how I receive new information about God. For example, I was raised to believe that God was the cause of all that happened. Both the good and the bad were within God's responsibility and reign. When, tragically, my best friend was killed in Vietnam, I held God immediately and totally responsible. I was in college at the time and was studying the New Testament. When the professor talked about the abundant love of God revealed in the parable of the sower (Luke 8:5-15), I had a difficult time listening. All the years I had spent knowing this loving God seemed to have vanished in light of my friend's death. This new experience of God as the "Cosmic Sadist" made thinking about God's love in class extremely difficult if not impossible. It was many years before I could "forgive" God for killing my friend and still many more before my theological understanding of God matured to the point at which I understood that the sinful state of humankind, not God, was responsible for John's death.

In the meantime, I struggled with each new insight about God that came through study in college and then in seminary. Reconciling the God I had known with the God I was meeting was hard work emotionally as well as intellectually. With each new revelation about God and God's actions in history, I was forced to reconsider not only my beliefs but my upbringing, not only my ideas but my parents' ideas, not only the church of the present but the church of my past. It was all up for grabs in light of my new learning.

A student of mine had a similarly disconcerting experience while in seminary, but for different reasons. She had been sexually abused by her father when she was twelve years old. Although it happened only once, the effects of the incident haunted her for many years. They also colored her relationship with God, whom she could no longer call "Father." She came to seminary because she wanted very much to be ordained. She was particularly eager to work with women who wanted to explore the connection between spirituality and sexuality. She was a very bright, articulate student who was eager to learn and quickly became a valued member of the community. She found the intellectual challenges of graduate level work to be stimulating and exciting and did well in her classes.

When she registered for the introductory course in New Testament, however, she ran into difficulty. Her study of the passages in which Jesus counsels forgiveness of those who have harmed us began to make her nervous. Prior to this point, she had not yet remembered that her father had abused her many years before. She only knew that she became agitated when she read passages about forgiveness (for example, Matthew 18:22, 35 and Mark 11:25). She also realized that she had difficulty praying The Lord's Prayer and now began to understand why. Jesus used the familiar *Abba* ("Daddy") to address God, but her experience of her father was distant and remote and filled with conflict and betrayal. She began to have flashbacks and gradually started to remember the incident in which her father abused and betrayed her. It was a shattering experience, and it brought her to my office in tears. After a lengthy conversation we agreed that she would seek professional help to address her new discoveries about herself and her history.

You would do well to spend time early in your seminary career thinking about the God of your youth. What did you learn about that God from your parents (whether or not you went to church)? We all generalize about God's attributes on the basis of our experience of life in our parents' home. What kind of parenting did you know growing up? Did you live with your parents or grandparents, or did someone else serve as your guardian? Was your home a peaceful place or one full of turmoil and abuse? Was your family intact for much of your growing up, or did you suffer loss one way or another and have to face debilitating grief that robbed you of your innocence and hope? Think about the answers to these questions. Then think about how your early ideas and beliefs about God were based on your answers to these questions.

Now think about your current ideas about God. If you were asked to describe God, what would you say? Such an exercise is important, for it can open up avenues for learning that might otherwise be blocked. For example, if I grow up viewing God as a demanding, judging, distant Being who watches my every move in order to trip me up and condemn me, I may find it difficult to examine ideas about God for long because that examination will bring me too close to God for comfort and safety.

COGNITIVE MAKEUP

Our cognitive makeup is also an important influence on the way we experience the classroom and whether or not we view learning as the enemy to our faith. Milton Rokeach did a study of cognitive approaches to learning entitled *The Open and Closed Mind*. As the title suggests, he identified two basic responses to learning that he called the open and the closed mind.[5] He understood that the learning task involves adopting

> a new belief system that is at odds with a previously held belief system. To deal with such tasks in terms of their intrinsic requirements entails a willingness to relinquish old systems, a capacity to entertain and enjoy new systems, and actively to synthesize new materials into an integrated whole.[6]

The mind that is receptive to new ideas and able to perform the primary tasks of learning (analysis and synthesis) with relatively little resistance or alarm belongs to the open-minded person, who is able to move into a new experience with anticipation and possesses the capacity to entertain new systems that are in opposition to familiar systems. The closed-minded person, in contrast, experiences greater anxiety in the face of new ideas and situations. He or she has difficulty with both analysis and synthesis because the old, closed system seems under attack. The perceived threat results in the closed-minded person frequently rejecting not only the new ideas but the person presenting them.[7]

Rokeach's insights are relevant to this discussion about theological education. In order for theological students to be prepared to offer the kind of informed, insightful, pastoral, and prophetic leadership needed in the church of the twenty-first century they must be fully able to grapple with highly complex questions, absorb and synthesize a vast amount of material from different but related fields of study, and become increasingly articulate about their own faith commitments as they are informed and shaped by their study. Students coming to this educational enterprise with closed minds will have greater difficulty in general when exposed to new ways of conceptualizing faith communities, new understandings of scripture, and new views on the role of the pastoral leader in today's rapidly changing church and society.[8]

Rokeach identifies one of the sources of closed-mindedness as one's view of one's parents. The open-minded persons in Rokeach's study showed more ambivalence about their parents and were generally influenced by others outside the family to a greater degree than the closed-minded people in his study. Rokeach theorized that the development of a closed system of beliefs may be a function of the breadth or narrowness of one's identification with others outside the family.[9] This breadth or narrowness would understandably be a function of the extent to which ambivalent feelings toward the parents are permitted in the family atmosphere. If I am not permitted to disagree or critique my parents, it is likely that I am in a family in which the parents are authoritarian and perhaps rigid in their own belief systems. If this were the case, I would probably grow up looking primarily to my parents and not others for guidance and direction. Rokeach's research shows us that our prior experience shapes not only our emotional response to life but our cognitive ability to assimilate new ideas as well.

I invite you to think again about yourself as a student of life. Do you tend to welcome new ideas and be eager to engage others in critical dialogue? Do you find new ideas difficult to entertain? Do you find yourself becoming anxious at the thought of being confronted with the need to change your belief systems based on new information? Do you find yourself in the middle of these extremes depending upon the subject matter?

THE NATURE OF EDUCATION

Billions of dollars are spent each year on programs of formal education. In some towns, the level of conflict and hence excitement in the local school board meetings rivals anything seen on television. Parents take their children's education very seriously as a rule and can be quite opinionated about where their tax dollars go relative to it. The past decade has seen a dramatic rise in the number of families home schooling their children in response to perceived deficits in the standard curriculum of the local public schools. This parental interest and investment in elementary, secondary, and higher education is good news for society in general, for studies have shown that the primary indicator for students' success in school is parental involvement.

A citizenry that is concerned about education is important, for education is one of the most powerful and relevant means for the transformation of society at our disposal. In the book *Higher Education as a Moral Enterprise,* Edward Long Jr. brings a critique to the academic enterprise as it has been shaped over the past forty years. He notes that while the cognitive dimensions of learning have received the lion's share of attention, there are other equally important dimensions that need the academy's attention as well. He argues that the purposes of higher education are cognitive competence and the formation of personal selfhood and social responsibility in the learner.[10]

Long's views about education are relevant to theological education as well.[11] Theologically educated persons are in touch with societal trends and technology; have a thorough and intimate knowledge of themselves as thinking, feeling, embodied, and spiritual beings; and evidence deep and firm commitments to a faith tradition that is at once rooted in the past, relevant to the present, and linked to the future.[12] In Long's terms, their education will have formed them into people who are cognitively competent, self-aware, and socially engaged and responsible people.

There is little doubt that as a society we value the educational process and view it as the means to a better life for individuals and society as a whole. In the same vane, the process of theological education is necessary for those who hope to be in some kind of ministry after graduation. Such an education must not stop short of tending to students' spiritual lives alongside their intellectual ones. To do so is to offer at best a truncated experience of intellectual and spiritual formation and at worst suggest that while faith without works may be dead, the head without the heart is just fine. Regrettably, not all seminaries are as intentional as they should be about helping students explore issues of their own faith formation and spiritual lives in tandem with their academic work.

Joseph C. Hough Jr. and John B. Cobb Jr. offer a critique of modern theological education in their book *Christian Identity and Theological Education.* In their chapter on "The Education of Practical Theologians" they write:

> In contributing to the education of the church's leaders, the seminary has the opportunity and responsibility to contribute to the understanding and practice of discipleship. This includes a concern

for deepening and clarifying the commitment to discipleship in ways that neither the scholarly study of subject matters nor the training in skills has done....Ideally, much of the legitimate criticism of the seminaries' spiritual aridity will be dissipated when the curriculum is reordered to promote discipleship.[13]

The promotion of discipleship ought to be the concern of every theological faculty regardless of the faith tradition to which they belong. The path to active discipleship will be different for each student, however, depending upon the shape of each one's faith commitments upon arrival at seminary. In the February 7-14, 1996 issue of *The Christian Century,* Miroslav Volf writes about theological education and the challenges facing a professor in such a context.

Volf describes the student who arrives at seminary with little, if any, prior knowledge of or experience in the traditions of faith composing the ecumenical Christian community. He points out that in the case of this student, the task confronting the teacher is somewhat different. A student without prior knowledge of and experience in the church will not even have the right questions to ask. There is nothing that can replace the cumulative effect of years lived in the church community. Indeed, without such a background, theological students are hampered from the beginning for it is difficult to think critically about questions of faith if one does not have a faith clearly formed with which to begin. This student, Volf says, needs to be led *into* the tradition.

Volf then writes about another kind of student and the consequent pedagogical challenge facing the professor.

How does one teach students who are deeply committed to the Christian way of life, have read a good deal of the Bible and know some of the tradition but are locked into misusing the Bible and tradition as ready-made blueprints for ordering life? If I need to lead the first kind of students *into* the tradition, I need to lead this second kind, in a sense *out of it*—that is, out of his [or her] own understanding of the tradition and of how it bears upon life today.[14]

Which kind of student are you? Do you come to seminary with years of lived experience in the church? Are you familiar with the biblical witnesses of the Hebrew and Christian covenants? Does the lexicon of the church make sense to you? Do you understand the meaning of terms like Advent, Lent, atonement, salvation, and justification by faith? Do you bring with you a rich background in the community of faith and countless Sunday worship services spanning your childhood and youth and young adulthood? Do you have some understanding of what it means to be faithful in the world because you have served on mission committees in congregations that gave witness to their love of Christ through service?

Or have you come to the Christian faith recently, perhaps during or after your college years? Did you attend church as a child and then drop away from it for various reasons? Have you come to your faith commitment after serious searching of yourself and the great religions of the world? Have you been a follower of one of these religions (non-Christian) and recently decided that the Christian faith is the one for you? Or after years of being a humanist or an atheist or an agnostic, and having discovered a deep longing for some connection with Something greater than yourself, have you come to seminary to find it?

ELEMENTS OF LEARNING IN THE CLASSROOM: CONTENT

Several dimensions of classroom experience contribute to your total learning in seminary. Course content itself, the pedagogical assumptions behind the design of the course, and your experience of God affect what and how you will learn.

Curricula in Protestant seminaries today are arranged in a variety of ways. Disciplines are organized into areas of study, sometimes called divisions. Generally speaking most courses offered are in one of the following areas: biblical studies, church history, ethics and theology, church and society, and pastoral theology. Schools differ on the number of credits required to graduate as well as the distribution of those requirements.

In the area of **biblical studies** you will be introduced to the sacred texts of the Hebrew and Christian covenants. You were probably raised to call these texts the Old and the New Testaments. If you are in a school that refers to them with different nomenclature than you are used to, you may confront your first challenge when you register for classes and are not sure where to find Old Testament and New Testament studies. Some scholars writing in today's climate of increased sensitivity to language and diversity believe that the language of "Old" and "New" suggests one covenant (the "new" one) is better in some important way and want to move away from the possibility of a pejorative term.

If your Bible faculty has made this decision, I hope that you will not allow yourself to be put off by it. Such a change may indicate an openness to diversity and expression that will in the long run be beneficial to you as you seek to learn to minister in an increasingly complex and diverse society and world.

In biblical studies you may expect to be introduced to methods of exegesis and ways of understanding scripture called "criticism" (form, literary, and redaction). As you become better able to do exegetical work, you will be able to understand what a given passage meant when it was originally written by studying the *Sitz im Leben* (life situation) of the text. Your study will enable you to move beyond a literal understanding of scripture to a more informed and comprehensive understanding of the life, times, culture, and belief systems of those who were inspired to write of God's activity in their lives and in the world.

Studies in **church history** will put you in touch with your forebears in the faith. You will see that they struggled to be faithful followers of the way of Jesus Christ through times of great societal upheaval and change. You will study the creeds of the church written in defense of orthodox understandings of the Godhead and in response to opposition sometimes named heresy. Through your study of the life and thought of the church you will see that there is not much new under the sun in the human condition. People still wonder about God, still struggle to make the church relevant to the times and issues and problems of the day, still need to find new ways to interpret for others the life-saving power of the gospel of Jesus Christ.

In **ethics and theology** you will study different ethical theories and examine your own ethical views and positions in ways that are new and perhaps challenging for you. You will consider what it means to have a consistent ethic out of which you live and minister, and you may even find that you need to become more consistent yourself. In the course of your study of ethics you will no doubt be expected to do a thorough self-study of sorts. I have heard from students over the years that the basic ethics course is one of the most difficult courses they take. Although some of that is no doubt due to the high standards of the professor, I believe most of the difficulty comes with the self-evaluation engendered by the subject matter itself. I cannot study ethics without also studying how it is that I make decisions, what my values and attitudes toward others are, and how my decisions affect others both for good and for ill.

You will probably be required to take a course in **systematic theology,** in which you systematically look at the three persons of the Godhead and consider the doctrines of the church that have arisen in response to God's saving activity in the world. If you did not study theology in college or have not done any in-depth reading in the area, you may find your head spinning as you consider the different doctrines of the church and learn its lexicon. Providence, creation, sin, salvation, redemption, atonement, and sanctification are terms used frequently in the church. You no doubt have heard them before, especially if you have spent any time in the church. Your study of them in seminary, however, will allow you to consider them in much greater depth. It will also enable (and perhaps force) you to wrestle with the meaning of the words for your own life and faith. The process of examining your own faith commitments as they have knowingly or unknowingly been shaped by the essence of these doctrines may be an exhilarating or a challenging process. Whatever kind of process it is for you, be assured that it is a necessary process. Without the hard work of study and self-examination that a course in systematic theology requires, you will be unable to preach and teach in ways that are grounded in the tradition yet alive to the contemporary church and world.

Anyone who expects to offer relevant leadership in the church of today and tomorrow must be a student of society: its cultures, customs, mores, and trends. To be able to offer the kind of transforming ministry needed so much in today's world, you will need to be able to do a sociological analysis of the community in which you serve and the congregation which you lead. Courses in the area of

church and society (sometimes called **religion and society** or **sociology of religion** or **church and community**) will enable you to understand the dynamics of change in the cultures of the sacred and secular world and bring a critical eye to your evaluation of the church as it is at present in a given community. Pastoral leaders of the future will, as always, need to be able to forge effective and lasting links between their churches and the community and its agencies in order to broaden the base of the church's effective witness and outreach. Studying in this discipline will enable you to not only foster solid links between your local church and the community but also to think about society and its ills from a sociological perspective that will inform your preaching and administration.

Courses in **pastoral theology** will introduce you to what some call the *basics* in ministry. **Preaching and worship, pastoral care and counseling, teaching,** and **administration** will probably be required courses in your Master of Divinity degree. Depending upon the school you are attending, there may be an equal or unequal balance of theory and practical experience in the courses themselves. Some schools have preaching and teaching labs in which you will be able to view yourself teaching or preaching by using a videotape recorder. At times you will no doubt be asked to report on your work in a ministry setting in relationship to class. For example, you may be expected to prepare a verbatim (report of a conversation you have with someone that is written down word for word as best you can remember it and analyzed along specific guidelines) of a conversation you have with a hospitalized parishioner.

You may have a tendency to view these courses as the "how to" courses and expect them to teach you all you really need to be a good pastor by telling you how to do it. Some students become impatient with time spent on the theory underlying the practice. For example, I have taught students in a course on death and dying who simply want me to tell them what to say to someone who is dying and not force them to spend weeks developing a working knowledge of the dynamics of grief and loss. Yet without the theory underlying that conversation with someone who is dying, they will soon run out of direction and will not know what to say. The theory is the road map. It provides the guidelines for effective work in response to the challenge of mortality and grief.

You may also be tempted to view these courses as being the ones that are really the most important ones in the curriculum. I have talked with some students over the years who put a substantial majority of their energy into the courses in pastoral theology, believing them to be the most important and directly relevant ones to ministry. This view is shortsighted, however, for it fails to recognize the role that the classical disciplines have in assisting you to learn to think critically and move between the abstract and its concrete application. Within this view also hides the spirit of anti-intellectualism, which opposes the ministry of Jesus Christ. To put it bluntly, it says, "Just tell me how to do it, I don't need to know how to think about doing it." At best this view is shortsighted; at worst it sets the stage for a shallow ministry that is incapable of understanding church and society in depth.

Having met the requirements of your particular degree program, you will then be able to take **elective courses.** Work closely with your adviser as you make your course selections, and avoid simply taking courses that match your time availability. Although I am fully aware of and somewhat sympathetic to the needs students have to schedule classes around very full and complex family and work schedules, it is a mistake to make choices that way all of the time. Students who do so fail to take seriously their investment of time and money in a degree that is to put them on the road to effective ministry across the years.

Instead of this shortsighted method of course selection, work with your adviser to plan an elective curriculum that will enable you to confront your weaknesses and work to eliminate them. For example, if you are new to Christianity and have come to seminary to establish your own faith commitments, you might consider taking more than one course in biblical studies. If your basic work in ethics and theology was extremely difficult for you, then perhaps you need to do more work beyond the basic requirements in these areas. If you plan on ministry in a hospital or other chaplaincy setting, you may need to take elective courses in psychology and religion. Let your areas of weakness and your vocational plans, not your schedule, dictate your elective selections.

Depending upon your school, you may be encouraged to take courses in any number of more contemporary theologies, such as feminist, womanist, and liberation theologies. Even if you do not come from a group that has given birth to a particular kind of theology (for example, you are not an African American woman drawn to womanist theology), I hope you will avail yourself of the opportunity to take at least one course in a theology with which you are unfamiliar. To do so will broaden your perspectives and assist you to adopt another frame of reference for a short while. It will also give you the chance to grow spiritually as you allow yourself to be vulnerable (that is, recognize that your way of believing is not the only legitimate way to believe) and humbly learn from others who may see things quite differently. Such an experience will assist you to become a better listener to others as well as to yourself, an invaluable asset in any form of ministry.

Your adviser may urge you to expand your horizons by taking advanced courses in curriculum development in multicultural settings, pastoral care and forms of addiction, or world religions and political ethics. Most seminaries offer a splendid array of elective courses from which to choose and more interesting things to learn than can possibly be absorbed in a finite time. I have heard more than one student lament that "there are so many good courses and so little time!" No doubt you will find this to be true in your seminary as well.

View the choices before you as a smorgasbord of the richest kind, a buffet of offerings that will continue to feed and enrich you. Although you may have obligations beyond studying full time, resist the temptation to take the expedient route and instead choose the courses that will make the best contributions to your broadly based preparation for ministry.

ELEMENTS OF LEARNING IN THE CLASSROOM: PEDAGOGY AND FORM

You can expect to have your courses meet in different formats depending upon the size of the enrollment and the nature of the subject matter. Some of your courses will probably be standard lecture courses, with some discussion time built into each session. Professors may choose to require additional class meetings that are discussion groups in order to allow students to be in dialogue with the professor, the material, and each other in a way that a lecture format will not allow. Readings and assignments will vary depending upon the professor and the class. You can expect, however, to have at least several hundred pages of reading assigned per week. A good rule of thumb to help you plan your schedule is to allow for two hours of preparation time outside of class for every one hour of time spent in class.

Some of your classes will probably be smaller in size and may be called seminars. Seminars usually are limited to 15 students who must have satisfied stated prerequisites before entering the course. Often seminars are upper-level courses in which students are expected to take more active teaching roles themselves. You may be required in a seminar, for example, to do a major paper and present it in class on a given day. It may be your responsibility that day to teach the class, presenting the material and leading the class discussion as well. Such an experience is helpful in many ways. The role of the teacher is a critical one for pastoral leaders; it requires ease in front of groups, familiarity with complex material, and comfort in holding authority. Presentations in seminars are good practice for seminarians who will one day be teachers in ministry.

Faculty are increasingly offering team-taught courses that cross disciplinary lines. You may be able to take courses, for example, that combine material on preaching and pastoral care or ethics and sexuality. Such team-taught courses model the kind of blending of material and perspectives that is an important skill for pastoral leaders, who must be able to do the same kind of thing as they think about issues of ministry and direction for church and society. When you are in full-time ministry, you will need to be able to gather insights from medical science and history, literature and sociology and to blend them into a coherent statement about where we are and where we need to go. Team-taught courses offer models of teamwork and thinking that are directly relevant to that task.

Another type of class will engage you in experiential learning situations. In addition to your experience in supervised ministry (or field education as it is often called) you will no doubt be asked to move beyond the narrow walls of your classroom from time to time and immerse yourself in real-life situations related to the issues raised in class. For example, when I teach a course entitled "Pastoral Care in Situations of Death, Dying, and Grief," I take my students to a local hospice for the day. Throughout the day students meet with patients, family members, and hospice staff to learn from them about the particulars of life and death in the hospice program. Such an experience pushes students to confront their own fears about dying and grief in a unique way. The profound encounter that takes place in this environment is qualitatively different from anything that can happen in the sterile classroom, regardless of my skill as a teacher, because the students have been brought face-to-face with death through the patients, family, and staff.

The faculty of Drew Theological School has long known the benefit of hands-on learning situations. For the past several years we have engaged students in learning situations through a program called The Newark Project. Students choosing to do so may take some of their required courses in the Newark track. Each of the courses related to the project puts students in appropriate field sites in the city of Newark, New Jersey. Students spend time with AIDS patients, work with women and children in battered women's shelters, care for drug addicts, and visit multiple community agencies, all under the watchful eyes of seminary professors and field supervisors. In addition, their concurrent work in Newark churches links them with religious bodies as well as community service groups.

The Newark Project has profoundly affected students who otherwise might never have so carefully considered the particular societal problems they encountered in the course of their studies. I recall the words of one student who had taken two courses through the Newark track. She said simply, "These courses have changed my life." When I asked her what she meant, she said that her middle-class upbringing had shielded her from the harsher realities of life. The insulation she grew up with, she now saw, had contributed to her failure to really understand what Jesus meant when he talked about "the least of these" because she had never really spent any time with anyone who would qualify for that title.

Your seminary may or may not offer these kinds of experiences within the boundaries of its courses. If it does, I hope you will seize the opportunity to learn in this way. To do so in the protected environment of the class and under the trained and watchful eye of your professor will guarantee that you will be broadened in necessary and lasting ways. Talk with your adviser about which courses offer this kind of experience, and take advantage of this part of the buffet—you will be glad you did.

Another kind of learning experience offered through many seminaries is **Clinical Pastoral Education (CPE).** CPE is offered around the world at centers accredited by the Association of Clinical Pastoral Education, headquartered in Decatur, Georgia. Students taking a unit (or quarter) of CPE must successfully complete at least 400 hours of supervised clinical work in an institutional setting (hospital, prison, nursing home, parish). The 400 hours will include small-group work in a peer group made up of your supervisor and fellow students, clinical interviews with patients (or prisoners or parishioners), didactic presentations on a variety of relevant topics, and frequent individual supervisory sessions with your supervisor who is also accredited by ACPE.

CPE is a grueling learning experience, but one that is well worth the time and energy required to complete it. Should you choose or be required to do a unit, you will have the opportunity to consider issues of ministry at the same time that you undertake a thorough and ongoing evaluation of your effectiveness as a pastoral caregiver. This preparation will enable you to better understand yourself, know and respect your boundaries, and discern and appreciate your emotions and their influential role in your ministry. At the same time, an experience of CPE will dramatically enrich your on-campus course work as you bring the learning of the clinical setting to bear on the material presented in class. For many students it is a life-changing experience.

As seminary faculties grapple with what it means to bring an effective and faithful witness to the gospel in today's world, we are seeing increasing numbers of schools require a cross-cultural experience for all Master of Divinity students. Although course titles vary from school to school (*transcultural, cross-cultural,* and *immersion experiences* are all common nomenclature), programs usually contain the following: on-campus course work prior to traveling to an off-campus site; a two-to-three-week immersion experience in the field; debriefing meetings on campus following the experience; and written work to summarize the learning.

While some programs dictate that students live in dormlike facilities, others allow them to live with the people from the area they are visiting. Students traveling to the Philippines, for example, may be able to live in the homes of Filipino people while they are in the country. Such an arrangement dramatically increases the learning opportunities, as students converse with families over meals and at various free times during the day and evening. It also allows for increased contact with the children and youth of the family when they are not in school.

Whatever the living arrangements, such a cross-cultural experience puts students in the vulnerable position of being in the minority, not knowing the customs, and perhaps not even knowing the language. This vulnerability enables them to look with new eyes at the customs of their own culture and church and to forever after bring a critical eye to "the way we always do things." If you are fortunate enough to participate in such an experience, you will be helped to mature spiritually as you are forced to rely more heavily on your travel group for survival and less on yourself. You will realize that the peoples of your host country have found effective ways to live and witness under very different circumstances. This, in and of itself, will provide an antidote to any temptations you may have to view your culture and ways of believing and doing things as categorically better or the only practical or legitimate way of living.

A final type of course being offered with greater frequency in theological education today is the church-based course. Such a course recognizes the quality of leadership (both lay and ordained) in given churches and links the seminary with the church in another type of team-teaching arrangement. Students visit the church several times throughout the semester and spend time discussing issues with the laity and clergy while there. In some situations, seminary professors join a pastor in team teaching a class at the church, which is open to laity and seminarians alike. These opportunities are exciting because they introduce you to effective and viable models of ministry while they also challenge you to bring a critical eye to the discussions about the church.

ELEMENTS OF LEARNING IN THE CLASSROOM: MEETING GOD

From the above summary of the kinds of courses you will probably be taking, you can see that a thorough course of theological study requires exposure to a wide variety of issues and perspectives, a combination of critical thinking and reflection on practice and a sustained look at oneself, one's values, and one's beliefs. All along the way you must also be thinking about and nurturing your beliefs and faith commitments.

The combined study of theology and ethics, church and society, experiential learning and cross-cultural studies forces students to examine and reexamine their own biases, beliefs, lifestyles, and values in profound ways. A corollary to this process is, of course, the exploration of the Godhead. Put simply, it is not enough in seminary for you to learn about God; you must also meet God. I cannot, for example, sit as someone preparing to be a pastoral leader in a class on contemporary social problems and trends without asking myself what God wants and how God views society today. As I answer those questions, I must also ask how God views me and how God is calling me to change.

This meeting of God occasionally proves difficult for students because sometimes the God they meet is not the one they had expected. Having grown up in a white, middle-class family, which was by most standards economically comfortable and secure, it was a relatively new idea for me that God's option is for the poor. Of course I knew that God loved the poor as God loved me and that God expected me to love them in active ways as well. The more comprehensive study of the gospel I undertook in seminary, however, showed me that God's love of the poor is an active choice that mandates certain behaviors and attitudes for me and for society that were not fully in place in my life. These behaviors and attitudes were not simply nice ideas, they were at the heart of the gospel. I had no choice about being engaged in caring for the "least of these"; if I wanted to call myself a Christian, then I had to work more actively to alleviate the ravages of poverty in its many forms.

Do not be surprised if you have a similar experience. We often create God in our own image, boxing God in and making God smaller than God is. Indeed, one of the tasks of the pastoral leader is to assist people to broaden their view of God as the One who flung the stars into the skies and created the universe as well as the One who cares for the tiny sparrow and clothes the lilies of the field—and the One who always cares for the least of these.

When you feel yourself being asked to stretch, resist the temptation to dig in and cling to your childhood notions about God. Instead, pray in earnest that God will be with you through this time of change and will help you to grow up in the faith to more mature and appropriate understandings of God and God's activity in the world.

Not all seminaries are equally prepared to help students think about and talk about their evolving faith. Some schools emphasize intellectual development over spiritual formation. In those cases students will need to find their own avenues to process new learning in light of their preexisting faith. Regardless of your seminary's views on the proper role of theological education in a student's developing faith, your seminary experience will have a profound impact on you as a believer. Put simply, theological education is not only an occasion for learned scholars to impart information. It is also an occasion of formation for students. The question to be asked, therefore, is not Is this school about the business of the formation of faithful disciples of Christ? it is, instead, What kind of formation is being offered?

STUDENTS SPEAK

In preparation for writing this chapter, I met with several first, second, and third year Master of Divinity students. Meeting with each class separately, I asked them the same question: "How has your classroom experience so far enhanced and detracted from your sense of yourself as a thinker and believer?" Their answers revealed a process of both intellectual and spiritual change and maturation. This change had not always come easily or quickly, but nevertheless, it had come. I include some of their comments here, expecting that you will be able to identify with them.

From the first-year students who had been in seminary for six weeks, I heard the following:

> The classroom is enhancing my spiritual growth, but it is separate from my faith life. That is not upsetting; it is just that the lecture format doesn't let me think about my faith that much.

> I can't integrate my classroom experience with my church, and that bothers me even though I was warned about it in my Old Testament class. I feel bifurcated, and I don't like it. . . . I'm learning that it is OK not to know and have all the answers. This is fostered in the classroom when we ask, "Why did this happen?" and the professor says, "We don't really know."

> I came to seminary with a view of God as omnipotent, and that is really being challenged here. . . . I have gotten in touch with my own need to know and have all the answers. I realize that I won't know everything, and that is starting to be OK. [When I asked him why he was changing, he replied: "I'm much bigger and deeper than I was before. . . . As long as we earnestly seek God's grace it comes."] It is very painful for me to rework old ideas about God and myself, but I believe that the pain here is purposeful and intentional.

> I came to seminary because God called me, but if God would just tell me I don't have to be here, I would leave! I am amazed at what I hear in class, and I wrestle with it because some of it is contrary to what I believe. I pick and choose from what I hear and pray for God's will to be done. I try not to be distracted from what God wants and I am still in constant dialogue with God.

> I came to seminary with an identity crisis and am trying to figure out what God wants me to do with my life. Some of what I am learning makes sense, but I don't see how it applies to my life yet. . . . I was expecting more of a spiritual quality to the classroom and not all of my professors start class with prayer.

These fledgling seminarians were having their eyes opened to new ways of thinking and believing. Some of their expectations about seminary were being met; others were not. Their first six weeks of theological education had been a time of exhilaration and struggle, a time of confusion and hope. While they were forming meaningful relationships with their classmates and sharing their intellectual and spiritual struggles with them, they were not yet certain about all they were hearing from their professors. Some of them were not even sure they should listen to their professors at all.

The woman who said she would leave if only God would let her also said that she picked and chose from among the things professors said in class. When I asked her how she determined what to keep and what to discard, she replied that if something matched her understanding and beliefs she kept it; if it did not, she discarded it. The standard against which she measured all she heard was the standard of her preexisting faith and knowledge.

While not representative of all students in seminary, her pick-and-choose method is common. I have heard too many students say that in order to defend their preexisting faith they will simply parrot the professor, all the while not believing (or really listening to) a word he or she says. The educator William G. Perry Jr. correctly refers to this response to confronting the challenges of higher education as "gamesmanship."[15] Should you ever be tempted to play this game, I hope you will not allow yourself to do so. Such closed-mindedness is the antithesis of the kind of thinking and openness that is at the heart of the gospel and so very needed in pastoral leaders today.

Meeting with second-year students, I heard some equally interesting comments:

> I am grateful that things are beginning to make sense to me now. In my first year everything was challenged. Now it seems like I am down to the real work of connecting what I'm learning with real ministry.

> If have my "glasses on" a whole new world emerges. [She meant if she were open to learning.] My faith has been firmed up through new ways of seeing things.

> I was new to Christianity when I came to seminary. This whole experience has opened up Christianity to me. I'm glad I came.

> The challenges I've had have been helpful ones. People in parishes are as afraid as we are, and I see that what I am doing in the classroom is impacting what I do in my churches.
>
> The two worlds I live in (seminary and church) are starting to merge this year. I was stagnant and waiting to be fed passively. Now I find that I am eager to feed others and share what I have learned.
>
> I find my classes intellectually stimulating; there is lots of food for thought. But spiritually I am not getting as much help. Most professors do not start class with prayer, and I wish they did. Prayer sets a tone of hope and encouragement that you can get through, that there is a possibility of success.
>
> I find that still it is easier to change my thinking than to change my beliefs. I mull over what I hear in class, and that helps me to be more open to it. I am cautious because I do not want to be molded by my professors.

These second-year students were beginning to make sense of things, and order was beginning to emerge out of chaos. Because they had worked hard over the past year to come to some deeper understanding of themselves and their relationship to God, they were not as vulnerable to ideas that were foreign or frightening. Most of them had matured through the experience and had a greater certainty about their vocational direction and spiritual growth.

I met with a group of third-year students around the same time in the semester. Some of the group gathered were about to finish their course work midyear. Others had one semester left before graduation. At least one member of the group had taken nearly five years to finish the degree due to family problems and personal illness. Their comments revealed both an excitement about having been at Drew and an eagerness to move on into full-time ministry.

> I am not the same person I was when I came to seminary. There were times when the only reason I stayed here was because my conference said I had to if I wanted to be ordained. I was challenged in my faith; my theology has turned around. I have been compelled through the discipline of study to become a deeper thinker. . . . God makes more sense to me now, even though I came to seminary with a close relationship with God.

God has taken on a new personality for me. God is no longer *out there*. The only way God is here is by us doing what the Holy Spirit empowers us to do. Christianity has been too preoccupied with personal piety....Now I will have to do battle with others back home in my church so that they stretch, too. This experience has put me in conflict with my church.

I've seen God in my class in the Newark Project when I was assigned to an HIV patient.

I came here hoping to be stretched farther, but it hasn't happened. Sometimes I am disinterested in class because I have heard it before. The Religion and Social Process class was one of the most inspiring classes.[16] It was interesting to look at how others have struggled with their own faith.

My faith was very threatened by the classroom. I never heard of form criticism, for example. It has been difficult to dialogue with professors because there is so much to cover in class. I could have used more help from the school in sorting it all out.

This experience has been a wonderful one for me. I am from Zimbabwe and am an ordained elder there. I am so happy to be able to study here. Many things I heard were not new to me but were challenging from a new culture....I have grown in my relationship to God....Sometimes the path to unknowing is the path to God.

When I met with this group, I was struck by their maturity. Unlike their struggling first-year colleagues, who were confused and excited at the same time, these folks seemed more stable and centered. Through the rigorous and demanding course of study they were soon to complete they had learned not *what* to think but *how* to think critically and with sophistication. They had learned not *what* to believe but that it is important *to* believe. They had learned about God and had also *met* God in important and life-changing ways. And they had been offered the chance to rely less on themselves and their own resources and more on the community God had created and given them in seminary and in the church at large. One third-year student, who had come to seminary from an abusive marriage with her ability to trust and form intimate relationships severely damaged, said

I have learned here that we all belong. I know now that we are all responsible for each other's salvation. I am much more aware of my neighbor than I was before I came to seminary. We are partners with God; I didn't know that before I came to Drew.

Her words of grace were a good summary of her seminary experience. She had a spiritual renewal, primarily a result of her classroom encounters with God in the learning community at Drew.

THE OPPORTUNITY OF CRISIS

The theological education you have undertaken is clearly a demanding pathway to preparedness for ministry. You can expect to be challenged physically, emotionally, intellectually, and spiritually. One way to view theological education is as a time of extended crisis in that you will find yourself and your prior ways of being and believing coming under review and ceding to new ways on an almost daily basis. This is as it should be, for any worthwhile program of theological education will be a program that assists (and sometimes pushes!) you to mature and "grow up in every way into him who is the head, into Christ" (Ephesians 4:15).

Just as God has created each one of us in unique and wonderful ways, so too, we respond to crisis in unique ways. Depending upon who you are and what your personality is, you may find that you welcome the challenge and change seminary brings, or you may resist it. Because we do not usually adopt new ways of coping in crisis situations but instead cling to past ways of coping, you can expect yourself to react to seminary in much the same way you have reacted to other times of upheaval and crisis in your life.

Take some time to think about yourself and how you have coped in the past. Do you usually remain open to the challenge of change? Do you try new behaviors on for size, so to speak, and examine them in a nonthreatened and nondefensive way? Or do you usually resist any effort to change at any level, dig in your heals, and turn the other way? Allow yourself to be honest as you do this bit of soul searching. Knowing the answer will help you make decisions about how you will react in class when you hear things that are new and different from what you previously thought. It will also give you the opportunity to more intentionally seek God's help in remaining open to the educational process.

HELP FROM SCRIPTURE

When we encounter God we are usually profoundly changed, even if we do not know it. If we stay in relationship with God, we are changed in predictable ways over time. Paul tells us the same when he talks about the fruits of the Spirit: "By contrast, the fruit of the Spirit is love, joy, peace, patience, kindness, generosity, faithfulness, gentleness, and self-control" (Galatians 5:22-23b). The Holy Spirit never comes into a life empty-handed. God always brings gifts and offers them in abundance. Paul has named for us several of the gifts God offers to those who are open to receiving them.

We cannot be with God without being changed for the better. As a result of my relationship with God, I have become more open to life and all that it brings my way because I have also become more secure in the knowledge that I am loved and that I am never alone. Such knowledge has brought with it a softening of my defenses over time and a maturity that allows me to be more open and tolerant of the shortcomings of others and myself. It also allows me to be more willing to entertain new ideas and points of view without fearing that my relationship with God will be challenged or harmed. Maturity in faith means that I realize that my rapport with God is not based on ideas about God but instead on my daily interaction with and devotion to God, who is the very "love that will not let me go."

THE WISDOM OF SOLOMON AND PAUL

When we think about the seminary experience and especially the classroom and its particular challenges to faith and intellect, we need to do so within the framework of scripture and what it tells us about God's desire that we learn about God and God's creation. Three scriptures have been particularly helpful to me as I have talked with students over the years about what it is like to be in seminary and how the material they are learning has affected them. The scriptures are: Proverbs 1:7; 2 Timothy 2:15; and Exodus 23:9.

King Solomon, author of the book of Proverbs, was a wealthy king, and the grandeur of his court was legendary. No doubt he dressed in the finest garments money could buy, for Jesus himself spoke of him as the epitome of beauty, which nevertheless paled in comparison to the lilies of the field clothed by God (Matthew 6:28-29).

For all of his wealth and power and luxurious living, however, he is most readily remembered as the source of many wise sayings. Who does not remember the story of the two women arguing over the baby in his court? When he declared that he would saw the baby in two and present each woman with half, he knew that the true mother would be revealed by her willingness to give up her son to save his life.

Such wisdom has caused King Solomon to be revered down through the ages as one of the wisest persons to ever live. The book of Proverbs is a collection of pithy sayings about wisdom and life that are still instructive to us today. This verse is the motto of the book: "The fear of the LORD is the beginning of knowledge; fools despise wisdom and instruction" (Proverbs 1:7). In this verse Solomon sets the premise for the rest of his reflections. The beginning and most important part of learning is the fear of the Lord. The word *fear* here means "reverence" or "awe." Solomon categorically states that there can be no true knowledge apart from God, neither can there be any true ethic apart from respect for the same God. Those who despise wisdom are foolish because they live without taking God into account and become morally corrupt in the process.

It is clear from this text that Solomon's worldview is centered in his understanding of God as the Creator of the universe and as the center of all life. Life makes sense only in that context, as does learning. Solomon's view is, for me, a breathtaking one, for he correctly links God and learning. God is not only the Creator of everything that lives; God is the One who has created us to be capable of learning in the first place.

As wonderful as God's gifts are, they always serve a purpose. Along with them comes the expectation that we will use them to the fullest extent for the betterment of the whole creation. Those who are wise realize this and actively seek ways to both understand the world through the use of their multiple gifts and to improve the living conditions wherever they find themselves.

King Solomon's ancient wisdom is true today: reverence for God is the beginning of all learning. The humble recognition that although God may be all-knowing, *I* am not spurs me on to learn more and more about God's world and my place in it. If I am spiritually alive, then it follows that I have a hunger to know God and God's creation in life-giving and redemptive ways. In contrast, if I say I am spiritually alive but remain closed to new learning and other voices, I am deceiving myself as surely as if I say I love God and despise my brother or sister (1 John 4:20). To reject learning, to be closed to a process of thinking about creation and its history, is to be removed from God in a certain sense. And it is spiritual arrogance that not so subtly declares that I already know all I need to know and I do not need others to complete or complement my learning. Solomon said that such people were foolish. Keep Solomon's words in mind as you move through the semester.

The second scripture that is instructive at this point is 2 Timothy 2:15. In this letter Paul is writing again to the young Timothy and encouraging him in the ministry. The theme of the letter is holding fast to the revealed truth about the divinity of Jesus Christ and the atonement offered through his death and resurrection. In a time when believers were turning away from the true faith, Paul counseled Timothy to hold on to the truth and to be faithful in his ministry.

> Do your best to present yourself to God as one approved by him, a worker who has no need to be ashamed, rightly explaining the word of truth. (2 Timothy 2:15)

As one might expect, it was the educated people in ancient times who became priests, scribes, and leaders of the community. By definition, a minister of the gospel would need to be constantly learning and intellectually, as well as spiritually, alive and vigorous.

At least twice in his correspondence with Timothy, Paul reminds him of this and urges him to continually be a student of God and life. In his first letter to Timothy he wrote:

> Until I arrive, give attention to the public reading of scripture, to exhorting, to teaching. Do not neglect the gift that is in you, which was given to you through prophecy with the laying on of hands by the council of elders. Put these things into practice, devote yourself to them, so that all may see your progress. (1 Timothy 4:13-15)

Having himself been a Pharisee who had studied the law for endless hours, Paul knew that anyone exercising spiritual authority over others needed to be adept at thinking, current in reading, and articulate in speaking about things that defied definition and could not easily be explained. If Timothy were to succeed as a minister of the gospel, he needed to study hard and continuously. Indeed, the phrase "devote yourself to them" has been translated in the following ways: "be in them"; "sink yourself in them"; "let them absorb you"; and "live in them." Reading these phrases, one gets the picture of Timothy immersing himself in the study of the word and people of God through Jesus Christ, of giving himself up wholly to the process, and of being energized by it.

Through such hard work and study, Timothy would not need to be ashamed in any way, and he would be able to "rightly explain the word of truth." In 2 Timothy 2:15, the Revised Standard Version uses the words "rightly handling the word of truth" to translate a Greek word that is believed to have come from the root word meaning "handle." That word originally meant "to cut straight" and was a metaphor inspired by the farmer who cuts a straight furrow or a tailor who accurately cuts a pattern. A farmer who is unprepared, who does not understand the farm equipment or the nature of the soil to be turned over, and who has not done the necessary homework before putting hand to plow will more than likely do a poor job of planting a straight row. And woe to the tailor who does not make a good cut in the fabric for lack of proper training; once the expensive fabric is mistakenly cut, there is no turning back, for the damage is done! Likewise with the minister, Paul said. Timothy had to continually do the hard work of preparation and study while he also engaged in ministry. If he did not continue to do both, he would be unable to tell the difference between the truth and apostasy, and lives would be adversely affected in the process.

Paul's insights about the link between ongoing education and effectiveness in ministry are timeless. His advice is as relevant today as it was nearly two thousand years ago. Remember Paul's words as you move through each semester.

HOSPITALITY: THE KEY TO THEOLOGICAL EDUCATION

The third message from scripture that is helpful to our discussion is the message to practice hospitality. Passages in both the Old and the New Testaments reflect the understanding that God expects us to offer hospitality to the stranger in our midst. We are to put our own desires and needs aside and consider instead the needs of the person standing before us. Notice in this passage, Deuteronomy 26:12-15, that the needs of the individual Israelite were the last ones to be considered.

> When you have finished paying all the tithe of your produce in the third year (which is the year of the tithe), giving it to the Levites, the aliens, the orphans, and the widows, so that they may eat their fill within your towns, then you shall say before the LORD your God: "I have removed the sacred portion from the house, and I have given it to the Levites, the resident aliens, the orphans, and the widows, in accordance with your entire commandment that you commanded me; I have neither transgressed nor forgotten any of your commandments: I have not eaten of it while in mourning; I have not removed any of it while I was unclean; and I have not offered any of it to the dead. I have obeyed the LORD my God, doing just as you commanded me. Look down from your holy habitation, from heaven, and bless your people Israel and the ground that you have given us, as you swore to our ancestors—a land flowing with milk and honey."

The faithful Israelite was one who thought of the vulnerable ones in society before thinking of himself or herself. The faithful Israelite did so not simply because the law required it but because it was possible (in fact even desirable) that he or she practice empathy by imagining how the other felt. In the following passages it is made clear that not only were the Israelites supposed to offer hospitality to the sojourner, they were to identify with the sojourner because of their own history.

> [God,] who executes justice for the orphan and the widow, and who loves the strangers, providing them food and clothing. You shall also love the stranger, for you were strangers in the land of Egypt. (Deuteronomy 10:18-19)

> You shall not oppress a resident alien; you know the heart of an alien, for you were aliens in the land of Egypt. (Exodus 23:9)

Such identification meant that the people of Israel were open to the stranger and the sojourner in profound ways. They were not simply to open their homes to them; they were to be connected to them in the way that only comes when we dare to allow ourselves to feel what the other person is feeling. They were to "get inside the skin" of the stranger, to feel what they felt, to see the world through their eyes for a while, and to care for them in as many ways as they could.

The mandate to be open to the other and to care for the stranger is carried forward into the New Testament. Jesus was known for being kind to outcasts: Mary Magdalene, Zacchaeus, the ten lepers, the woman at the well, the woman with the flow of blood. The list is long of those he talked with and ate with and loved with the everlasting love of God. Had it been up to his disciples and the temple officials, he would not have mingled with the "least of these" as he was apt to do. In so doing, and in his instruction to love one another in the same way that he has loved us, he was clear that we are to practice hospitality wherever we find ourselves. That we may be surprised at the rewards is suggested by the author of Hebrews: "Do not neglect to show hospitality to strangers, for by doing that some have entertained angels without knowing it" (Hebrews 13:2).

My experience has been that students in seminary often fail to understand the full meaning of hospitality and its implications for spiritual life and growth. Depending upon their background, they may realize they are called to be open to people of other faith traditions and other racial or ethnic backgrounds. They may deliberately seek to understand their colleagues in class and try to listen carefully to others who view things differently. Their hospitality, however, is often a selective hospitality, offered when the risk to themselves is not high or their investment in the relationship not too great. When the opposite is true and their sense of themselves is threatened by the other, they may shut down and become inhospitable to the person or the experience or the idea.

These students in particular need to remember that the key to a theological education that has integrity and value is an attitude of hospitality. As we have seen, sometimes students view the enterprise as the enemy of faith. Such a view is shortsighted and ultimately harmful to one's ministry. If you find yourself in that position, you need to reframe your view of the seminary and see it as the avenue to greater faith that it really is. Do not allow yourself to abandon the rigorous intellectual work that is required; do not give in to any impulse to "tune out" the professor or your classmates because you do not like what you are hearing or are threatened by it. To quote Professor Ada-Maria Isasi-Diaz, Associate Professor of Ethics and Theology at Drew, "If theological education can kill your faith, your faith is not that strong!"

I once met weekly with a group of students in a covenant group. Early on in our time together I heard a lot about a required course that most of the members were taking at that time. With one exception, those in the group reported feelings of frustration with the class. They felt that their insights, expectations, and beliefs were ignored and looked down upon by the professor. Student after student reported a high level of stress over being in the class; they did not want to go and were in distress over the very thought of it.

I asked them to think about the spiritual challenge facing them in the experience and introduced the biblical metaphor of hospitality. While they saw the problem as the professor's failure to offer hospitality to them and their ideas, I saw it somewhat differently.

I challenged them to look within themselves to see how they were failing to offer hospitality to their professor, to the experience of the class, and to their own feelings.

Over the next three weeks we focused on this theme of hospitality, and their experience of this class and its professor began to change. Gradually they saw that they were guilty of inhospitable behavior and spiritual arrogance at the same time. Because they did not like what he was saying, they assumed he was wrong and had nothing to teach them. Instead of talking with him about their feelings and ideas, however, they were content to complain to me. I invited them to think about the practice of hospitality and what it would look like in relationship to the class and professor.

They began to realize that they needed to talk with him during and after class in order to better understand what he was saying. They also began to realize that through this process they could offer hospitality to him and to their own feelings.

When I am practicing hospitality, I am receptive to what comes my way and, in time, respond to it out of the storehouse of my own personal, intellectual, emotional, and spiritual resources. I do not automatically cut off dialogue or immediately build walls between myself and the other so that I will not be affected by the encounter. Were I to do so, I would be cutting myself off from life itself and banishing myself from a process of true learning and growth that only comes when I am open to the possibility of becoming a new creation in Christ on a daily basis. In other words, if I am inhospitable, I am closed to life and to God.

EXERCISE

For this exercise spend some time thinking about your experiences as a student. Who was your favorite teacher in elementary school? high school? college? What did that teacher do that was special? What did he or she teach you about learning and its importance in life? Think also about your parents' attitudes about learning and school. What did you learn from them in this regard? Think about the pastors you have known. What did they teach you about the importance of study and education in relationship to being a Christian and also to being ordained?

After you have spent some time thinking about all of this, turn your attention to yourself. What kind of student were you when you were in school? Did you enjoy studying, or did it seem like a chore with little joy attached to it? What was your most difficult subject? Why? How did you react when confronted with new material that was difficult? Did you like the challenge, or did you feel overwhelmed and discouraged by it? How do you react now as an adult learner in the same situation?

Finally, give yourself some time to think about the connection between your intellectual life and your spiritual life. Do you share John Wesley's desire that we

> Unite the pair so long disjoined,
> Knowledge and vital piety:
> Learning and holiness combined...?[17]

If you do not share this desire, why not? How might you move in that direction so that you recognize the intertwining of your intellectual life and your spiritual life?

Prayer: Beloved Friend, King David knew you as the one who traveled with him wherever he went. He wrote that you would be with me in my going out and my coming in, forever.[18] That is good news, for sometimes I do not know whether I am coming or going! I hear so many new ideas, I listen to so many different beliefs, I work so many long hours that I can lose my way, my perspective, even my close walk with you. Be for me the same abiding presence David knew. Give me the assurance that regardless of where my journey leads me, you are there by me, within me, guarding and guiding me. Help me to know that I never journey alone; rather, I travel in the company of my fellow students, the faculty, and the staff of my school. You have given us to each other so that we might help each other, teach each other, learn from each other. Keep me open to learning from this community of faith. Give me grace to be for others a loving presence along their way. And always hold me close to yourself, that I may be lifted up and strengthened and made fit to give faithful witness to your claim upon my life, now and always. In Christ's name I pray. Amen.

CHAPTER 6

The Practice of Ministry

You received without payment; give without payment. Matthew 10:8

y the time I was in college, I had already known for more than five years that I was going to pursue ordination in The United Methodist Church. I had been active in my home church all of my life and was eager to be in ministry full time. While in college, I worked on campus. It was through that job that I met and was "adopted" by the alumni director of the school and his wife. We had many long talks about my vocational aims, and I was helped and supported a great deal by their encouragement and wisdom. I recall one time in particular, during my senior year, when I became restless to be free of the bonds of a formal academic program and able to spread my wings and fly into full-time ministry. I looked into my future, and all I could see was an endless line of semester upon semester of study stretching out in front of me. It did not help that I was soon to graduate from college. Beyond that bright day loomed at least six more semesters of seminary study.

I began to despair of ever being ordained; it seemed a lifetime away and forever beyond my grasp. I shared my frustration one day with Dale in the hope that he could help me. I was not disappointed, for what he said helped me to be content with my status as a student, and I have repeated his words often to students in seminary. He wisely reminded me that although I still had a great deal of schooling left before I would be launched into the world of ordained ministry, it was equally true that I did not have to wait until then to be in ministry. In fact, I could be and was in ministry already—in the dorm when I helped a sister student, in the office when I finished a rush printing job, on campus when I met with the little sister assigned to me as an upper-class student, and when I taught the fourth graders each Sunday at the local church. Dale's words helped me not only to be patient but also to view my daily life with new eyes and to be satisfied.

The excitement and exhilaration about being in ministry is a common phenomenon in theological schools. Students usually come to seminary with an eagerness to be in ministry in the world so they can share the love of God and work for a more just society. Sometimes they come with an eagerness to learn; sometimes the formal learning process feels like an impediment to being in ministry. Whatever the case, few students disagree about wanting to be in ministry.

You may share this eagerness to be in ministry, and it is laudable. Yet your eagerness may have a negative effect on you if you are not careful. It may make you less open to material that does not obviously and automatically relate to your present or future setting for ministry. What, indeed, does the study of the first-century church have to do with ministry in the twenty-first century, which is fast approaching? How does the study of multiple forms of liturgy and styles of preaching apply to you when you will be going to a particular church that expects a particular kind of preaching from a particular kind of preacher?

Theological education is a demanding course of study, requiring not only long hours of study but also long "simmering hours" in which students can sit with the material and gradually have it come into focus and make sense. Yet too often I have seen students who undervalue their time spent in the classroom because they are eager to engage in acts of ministry in the "real world." Time spent in classroom work *is* connected with time spent beyond the classroom absorbing the material.

I once taught an introductory course in pastoral care in a two-week intensive format. The class met four days a week for three hours each day. By the end of the two-week period we had the requisite twenty-four contact hours. I compared this experience with other courses I had taught in a whole semester format and decided that I would not choose to do an intensive two-week course again. The subject matter required students to do considerable soul searching and to examine their families of origin in a new way. The skills of active listening and spiritual analysis were ones that they needed to practice for a long time. I concluded that the students in this two-week intensive course did not have enough time to sit with the material and absorb it.

I have also seen students take too many credit hours per semester in order to finish their degree and move into full-time ministry as soon as possible. Although I understand this eagerness, I caution you against taking what may be an unwise credit load and not fully benefiting from the educational process. It takes time to mature.

Supervised Ministry

One part of the curriculum that should help meet your very real need to be in service in the world at the same time that you are in classes is **supervised ministry.** It is considered such a vital part of seminary education that the Association of Theological Schools (ATS), the accrediting body of theological schools in North America, lists as one of its standards for accreditation the necessity of students engaging in the practice of ministry under competent supervision while they are in seminary.

Nomenclature for the program differs from school to school: Field Work, Field Education, Supervised Ministry, Contextual Education, or Practical Ministerial Training. Whatever the name of the program, it engages students in learning sites outside the classroom where they are in ministry, working closely with a mentor/supervisor.

Details of programs vary as do titles. Most schools require Master of Divinity students to work in churches for at least part of their time at seminary. In addition, some schools require students in be in a class on campus, in which they reflect critically on issues of ministry through an academic/theoretical lens, at the same time that they are in ministry settings. Such classes are designed to assist students to become theologians as well as more objective and informed thinkers about themselves and ministry.

The program at Drew Theological School, for example, is required of all Master of Divinity students in their second year of study. Students receive six academic credits (three each for the fall and spring semesters) for their work in ministry settings concurrent with their enrollment in a seminar that meets once a week for two and a half hours. Students' current practices of ministry launch the discussions, which focus on a variety of ministerial issues including students' metaphors for ministry, leadership styles and skills, conflict management in the context of the faith community, lay ministry in relationship to ordained ministry, and analyses of the congregations and communities in which students are serving. Through lectures, case study presentations, theological reflection, readings, and journaling, students are challenged in the ways they think about themselves and ministry, assisted to become more articulate in their theological understandings of ministry, and encouraged within a supportive small group context to try new skills in their ministry setting. Small groups are led by adjunct faculty, who are pastors, and full-time faculty serving as advisers for the current second-year class.

STRUCTURES OF ACCOUNTABILITY

Over the past twenty years there has been a movement in theological education to raise the quality of programs in field education. Structures of accountability are fairly uniform in most schools although the nomenclature differs. You can probably expect to have the following elements as part of the requirements of your field education program:

Learning/Serving Covenant
Supervision by a qualified mentor
Lay training committee
Evaluation process

Learning/Serving Covenant

Often there is a document called a Learning/Serving Covenant (LSC) or Learning Contract in which you will be asked to identify your learning goals for the experience as they are related to the actual work you will be doing. Most schools require that the LSC be developed through conversations among you, your mentor/supervisor, and selected persons in the ministry setting. This document serves as the operating agreement about how you will spend your time in the setting and what responsibilities and opportunities you will have there. It is usually understood to be a binding document, albeit a fluid one. Learning/Serving Covenants of Drew students may be changed, for example, if all parties agree to the changes; thus, we recognize that the needs of students and ministry settings may change over the course of the academic year.

Supervision by a Qualified Mentor

Supervision by a qualified person with many years of experience in ministry is a standard requirement of Field Education programs. The amount of supervision required will vary from school to school. Drew requires at least one supervisory session every two weeks and distinguishes between supervisory sessions and staff meetings. The latter involves all staff in the setting and focuses upon the upcoming program of the setting. Pastoral supervision, in contrast, takes place when the seminarian and the supervisor meet for an uninterrupted period of time without other staff members present. Expect your supervisory session to help you think more critically about acts of ministry; challenge you to evaluate yourself in light of new learning and feedback from your supervisor and others; and enable you to refine your skills as a pastoral leader and theologian through conversation with a more seasoned person in ministry. The relationship you have with your mentor/supervisor is a critical one. It combines elements of support, accountability, discipline, and apprenticing.

You will address a variety of issues with your mentor/supervisor such as:

pastoral identity and ethics
the nature of ministry
your call to ministry
the ordination process
authority issues
sexuality
time and conflict management
spirituality
church growth and discipleship

How we integrate each one of these topics in our lives has a profound impact on the ways we minister. It is important that you have the chance to discuss your own views about them with a more seasoned pastor.

I began working in a church during my first year in seminary, and I was excited and scared all at once. Though a lifelong, active church member who had assumed a variety of leadership roles, I had never been a pastor before. Immediately people treated me as if I knew more than I did, had lived longer than I had, and possessed more wisdom than I thought myself to have. What I needed desperately was someone who had walked the path I was now walking, who had also had a first day in ministry that was both exciting and frightening. I needed someone who could be a beacon in the now confusing world of ministry and who would guide me, care about me on the journey, believe in me, and help me to become the spiritual leader God had called me to become. I also needed someone who would challenge me intellectually and spiritually, and let me know when standards of performance were not being met.

All of these gifts are potentially present in the ideal mentor/supervisor. When you are asked to consider a particular setting, be sure to talk long enough with the person who will be your mentor/supervisor to be able to sense the fit between the two of you. Do you feel comfortable in her presence? Do you agree with his basic philosophy of pastoral leadership? Is this someone you like enough to want to have regular contact with? Do you admire the person and their work, reputation, and example as you know it?

Lay Training Committee

Over the past fifteen years in field education, we have seen a shift in understanding about the very nature of ministry. Vatican II and, more recently, theologies that have focused on the lived experiences of faith communities (such as feminist, womanist, liberation, black theologies) have helped theological faculties to broaden their understandings of the role of laity in the ministry of the church. Many seminary curricula reflect the understanding of the call to ministry through one's baptism; most field education programs do as well. Specifically, most schools have added the lay committee to their programs. Once again the names of this particular structure of support and accountability differ from school to school: Teaching Church Committee and Lay Training Committee are the most common.

The lay committee typically comprises six to eight laypeople drawn from the ministry setting in a representative way by virtue of age, knowledge of the setting, or position of leadership. Committee members understand themselves to be called to ministry by virtue of their baptism, want to help educate the seminarian for effective ministry, and are able to be both supportive and confrontational. They are willing to commit themselves to several regularly scheduled meetings throughout the time that the student is in the ministry setting. With assistance in agenda setting from the seminary, the lay committee focuses on the nature of ministry in that particular locale, the student's progress and formation as a pastoral presence and leader, and the revision of learning goals.

The lay committee has a variety of functions: feedback and support, formal evaluation, development of realistic and manageable learning goals, interpretation of the seminarian's work to the wider community within the setting, and liaison between the student and the church (or agency). It provides a net should the student fall and a context for conversation about issues that reflect both the life and concerns of the laity and the needs of the church for its pastoral leaders. Where else will a student be able to have regular and sustained conversation with a small, committed group of laity about important issues of faith and life in the church and world? The lay committee provides a safe place for the seminarian to discuss issues and concerns, dreams and disappointments, and hopes and fears about ministry, leadership, faith, and theology.

Evaluation Process

The final standard component of most field education programs today is the evaluation process. Once again, procedures vary from school to school. Some schools have their own printed evaluation form for supervisors and committees to use; others simply ask for a letter of evaluation from the supervisor.

Most schools will ask you to do an evaluation of yourself as a developing ministerial leader. This exercise is an important one, for effective pastoral leaders are able to evaluate themselves in an ongoing way and to make course corrections as necessary. If you have never been asked to evaluate yourself in a formal way before, do not assume you cannot do it. The exercise calls for prayerful and objective consideration of your efforts and accomplishments over the past semester or year. You will probably be asked to write about your strengths and weaknesses as you know them and to reflect on areas in which you need growth.

My experience is that students tend to be much harder on themselves than are their supervisors or lay committees. Usually they are quick to point out their deficiencies and slow to claim their growth and skill. Some of this comes from humility, a virtue to be sure. But some of it comes from having unreasonably high expectations that are doomed to be unmet. One of the primary benefits of the lay committee comes when students realize that others see them as gifted and productive people in their own right.

Any formal evaluation process should link the experience in field education to the rest of your academic work and preparation for ministry. Evaluation provides a window on areas in which you need to do further work. If you have difficulty with hospital visitation, then you may need to do a course in pastoral care and counseling. If your preaching is weak, you may need to take more course work in preaching or exegesis. If your interpersonal skills are not as good as they should be, you may need to take a unit of Clinical Pastoral Education (CPE). View the evaluation process as a gift that enables you to better chart your course through the curriculum and build on the gifts and graces God has already given you for ministry.

These, then, are the elements of a good field education program: class work applying theory to the student's concurrent practice of ministry; regular supervision by a qualified, experienced person; frequent, disciplined conversation with laity about issues in ministry; a Learning/Serving Covenant that addresses learning goals and job responsibilities; and a formal evaluation process that requires the student to evaluate himself or herself and to receive evaluation from others in the ministry setting. If these elements are in place, you can expect to have a field education experience that will be beneficial to you in your preparation for ministry and that will help you to make links between your academic work and the practice of ministry.

Sometimes the evaluation process leads to the logical conclusion that the seminarian should not proceed to ordination. When such a painful conclusion is reached, however, the supervisor and lay committee need to work closely with the director of the field education program to convey the word to the seminarian. Such an evaluation does not usually mean that the student is blocked from pursuing ordination within a given denomination. The ordination process is usually distinct from the granting of the academic degree in the Protestant church. If there is integrity to the evaluation process, however, the student should be lovingly assisted to seriously consider what is being said by the people with whom he or she has worked closely for nearly a year. Other kinds of ministry should be explored; sometimes a student is advised to enter into a counseling relationship in order to sort out the feelings and thoughts accompanying the evaluation process or exposed by it. The student's faculty adviser can be of help during this difficult time.

HUB OF CURRICULUM

Rightly viewed, the field education program is the hub of the curriculum for the Master of Divinity student. Course work in the areas of biblical studies, church history, theology, ethics, religion and society, and pastoral theology are all potentially directly related to the practice of ministry. I use the word *potentially* because not all seminaries are as intentional about linking the classroom with students' practice of ministry as they could or should be.

When faculty fail to take into account the fact that their students are already serving in ministry and therefore are in a position to use the classroom material readily and regularly, they are failing to exploit the ministry setting for the laboratory it really is. Exegesis on a given text in a New Testament class, for example, may be appropriately formatted for use in a devotional time during a meeting of the church council or in a Sunday sermon. Questions raised in a class on the early church may be relevant to a discussion the student is leading in her church about the mission of that particular local congregation as it struggles to redefine what it means to be a faithful witness at the beginning of the twenty-first century. Issues of diversity and racism raised in a class on religion and society may be used to do an analysis of the student's ministry setting and shared appropriately with the supervisor and laypersons there.

Viewing the curriculum as a wheel with field education at the hub, we see that the spokes make two way communication possible. Not only does classroom material apply to the work of students in ministry; the work of ministry infuses classroom conversations with meaning and depth that would be missing if the classroom existed in a vacuum apart from the lived ministry experience of the students. I hope you presuppose the link between classroom and experiential learning.

The goals of a quality field education program of contextual learning are to help the student become better informed and able to perform in ministry. Specifically, such a program aims:

1. To develop the leadership qualities and skills necessary to lead communities of faithful disciples of Jesus Christ into service in the world.

2. To gain in ability to perform the pastoral tasks as the student's tradition allows.

3. To grow in the ability to relate with integrity and constancy with people of all ages, races, and lifestyles.

4. To learn to do theological reflection and relate it to one's life and ministry.

5. To grow in one's own spiritual life and discipleship and become able to lead others to deeper faith commitments.

6. To gain clearer direction about one's chosen vocational path and wrestle with questions about ordination and its appropriateness for oneself.

LEADERSHIP

The central task of theological education today is to train leaders for the church and world. As the world has changed dramatically since World War II, so has the church. The women's movement of the 1960s and '70s has forever altered the ways our society views women and men and their roles in the culture and the family. The increasingly large number of women moving into the workforce over the last several decades has made it more difficult for them to find time for volunteering and community service. Couples struggling to make ends meet and to find time for children and each other often have little time to attend church meetings or work on committees.

Advances in medicine since World War II have extended the life expectancy for men and women to beyond seventy years. The same advances have brought with them difficult questions about life-support systems and their withdrawal, living wills, physician assisted suicide, and the appropriate use of limited natural and financial resources.

The burgeoning field of computer technology enables us to be connected in ways heretofore unimagined while at the same time it breaks down community by replacing face-to-face interaction with a sterile screen. Youth, now dubbed Generation X, have new ways of thinking, seeing, and processing information—along with new expectations for worship and fellowship. Many do not see the necessity of attending church or of being involved in any ongoing faith community. People of all ages are being affected by technology. We are growing accustomed to instantaneous answers and becoming more driven and work oriented.

Progress made through the Civil Rights movement and the leadership of the Reverend Dr. Martin Luther King Jr. is muted by the gang wars, hate crimes, and church burnings seen all too frequently in this country and around the world. Although our society has made progress in its recognition that "all men [and women] are created equal," not all members of our society enjoy equal access to the halls of power and influence, nor do they realistically expect that to change any time soon.

Society today is more complex, fast changing, and secularized compared to that of fifty years ago. Such changes are apparent in the church as well. Anyone wanting to become a leader in the church today must be focused, able to name and interpret societal trends, conversant in the use of technology, abreast of issues in medical ethics, and deeply committed to fostering relationships across racial and socioeconomic lines. The process of becoming such a leader is a challenging and exciting one; it is also a process that is central to the field education experience.

Your experience in the program should be one in which you are assigned responsibility for a given area of the program that will enable you to be accountable for the analysis, planning, implementation, and evaluation of ministry in that area. In addition, any quality field education setting will be viewed first and foremost as an opportunity for you to learn (as opposed to a way to fill a slot on the staff). Because that philosophy undergirds the program, you should be able to be involved in much more of the total ministry of the church or agency, as time allows and your interests and abilities dictate. Visitation, for example, is a good way for you to learn about pastoral care and issues facing senior citizens in your area.

Have you ever held a leadership position before? When? Where? What were you expected to do as the leader in that group? What was your leadership style like at the time? As you view society now, do you think you would need to make changes in your leadership were you confronted with the same set of issues and challenges today? Take some time to think about yourself as a leader now. Let your reflections help to shape your goals for your own development as a leader through your field education experience.

PASTORAL TASKS

Ordination in most cases assumes that the ordinand will eventually be officiating in the liturgical life of the faith community. Although some persons who are ordained go on to specialized ministries of teaching, chaplaincy, agency administration, counseling, and other worthwhile ministries, they should still be able to offer informed and careful leadership in the more public moments of ministry. All Master of Divinity students benefit from practice of the tasks of the pastoral office.

Preaching, teaching, administration, counseling, praying extemporaneously and in public, officiating at weddings and funerals, and organizing communities for social action and outreach are all necessary skills for one seeking ordination. Field education is designed, in part, to give you an opportunity to perform these tasks under the guidance of a skilled and experienced mentor/supervisor.

Have you ever preached before? If you have not, you should preach a minimum of three times during the academic year at your field setting. If you are fortunate enough to have preached before or are currently serving as a local pastor who preaches each week, you would do well to ask for specific feedback about your sermons and not simply assume that because you do it all the time that therefore you do it well.

Officiating at the time of a funeral is one of the most important tasks facing a pastor. It takes sensitivity and skill to be able to acknowledge grief appropriately while at the same time offering the hope of eternity through Jesus Christ. It takes practice to know when to offer words of comfort and when to encourage the grief, anger, fears, and hopelessness that usually accompany loss. If your ministry setting does not offer opportunities to perform funerals, you would do well to speak with your supervisor about it. Perhaps you and he or she might speak with a local funeral home director so that you can do services for the unchurched families in your area as the need arises.

The teaching office of the pastoral leader is a precious one. Bible study, sermons, pastoral newsletters, and public speeches are all occasions for teaching about the liberating gospel of Jesus Christ. Indeed, one might argue that the pastor is teaching at every moment; the only question is, therefore, What are you teaching through your interactions with others, your standards for your own work, the vision for ministry you offer, and the quality of your relationship with God through Jesus Christ?

Being a good teacher requires knowledge of learning theory, contemporary issues and questions, ability to move freely between the abstract and the concrete, and enthusiasm for the subject matter. A good pastor-teacher is one who loves God and people, believes the gospel of Jesus Christ, is careful enough to prepare lessons thoroughly, is current in societal issues and problems, is able to understand them theologically, and views the process of learning itself as a gift from God. It requires hard work to prepare Bible studies that are interesting and understandable. You can expect to need the same level of preparation, reflection, and study for a Bible study or adult education class as for a sermon.

Because the teaching office is so central to all a pastor does, you should take care to have teaching responsibilities as part of your field education experience. Ask to be assigned to a regular class as the teacher for the year. Volunteer to take part in leading a Bible study or confirmation class. Find ways to lead an adult class on current events or faith formation. You may need to be proactive in pursuit of teaching opportunities in your ministry setting. Having a teacher on your teaching church committee would enrich your conversations about the teaching role within the community of faith.

In order to keep the ministry of the church or agency moving along in a healthy way, it is necessary for the pastoral leader to be a skilled administrator. Analyzing issues and resources, training laity for the ministries to which they are called, delegating responsibilities in a timely and appropriate way, doing the necessary paperwork that is part of any organization, all are skills needed in pastoral leaders today.

I have too often heard students lament that they are facing considerable administration when they enter ministry. They tell me how they would much rather spend their time with people than with paper and how they will spend as little time as possible doing administration. I challenge them to reframe their view of administration, from the uninspired shuffling of paper to a way of organizing the love of the congregation. Structures, procedures, and committees all help the church to survive and thrive in a busy and complex world. They are necessary parts of the life of the church, the skeleton of the church on which the mission and program hang.

Your field education setting should provide you with administrative responsibilities so that you can study the methods of organization in that local situation, analyze them through the lens of efficiency and spirit of the gospel, and come to an awareness of your own administrative abilities.

In summary, your field education should offer you sufficient hands-on experience in the tasks of the pastoral office so that you conclude the program more capable and comfortable in those important roles. Make certain as you are planning your year in the setting, to negotiate sufficient time in each of these areas to ensure your participation in all of them as much as the setting and your time allow.

INTERPERSONAL RELATIONSHIPS

Members of a congregation will forgive a pastor just about anything as long as they know the pastor loves them. In other words, the pastor's relationship with the people she or he serves is of paramount importance.

You may have heard the saying that the gospel is not so much taught as it is caught. Paul understood this when he talked about being all things to all people for the sake of the gospel.

> For though I am free with respect to all, I have made myself a slave to all, so that I might win more of them. To the Jews I became as a Jew, in order to win Jews. To those under the law I became as one under the law (though I myself am not under the law) so that I might win those under the law. To those outside the law I became as one outside the law (though I am not free from God's law but am under Christ's law) so that I might win those outside the law. To the weak I became weak, so that I might win the weak. I have become all things to all people, that I might by all means save some. I do it all for the sake of the gospel, so that I may share in its blessings. (1 Corinthians 9:19-23)

Paul was eager to spread the good news of the redeeming love of Jesus Christ by whatever means necessary. In this section of 1 Corinthians, he is speaking about the nature of relationships. It is a fact of human nature that we listen more to people for whom we have a positive personal regard than to those whom we dislike. People we respect and like have far more influence over us than people we disrespect and dislike. Through the language and customs and worldviews of Jews, Paul made it easier for the Jews to want to listen to him. He did not seem a threat to them; on the contrary, he seemed like one of them in an important way. He got and held their attention through his relationship with them.

This dimension of relationships is true today. If we like and respect someone, we will be much more likely to turn to that person in times of need, listen to her ideas, be influenced by his values and faith system. This is certainly true of parishioners' relationships with their pastor.

I once knew two pastors. One was friendly and outgoing; the other was shy and withdrawn. The first pastor preached sermons that were well prepared on occasion but usually lacked the hard exegetical work necessary for a solid sermon. In addition to his general lack of preparation for worship, he was very loose administratively. He did little to promote the organizational systems of the church; what happened in terms of committee meetings was because of the initiative of the parishioners. His real strength was interpersonal relationships. He was a real "people person." He loved visitation; the children adored him; he was always available for counseling; and he was immediately on the scene when there was a death or a crisis.

The second pastor was a good administrator. He had his sermons planned months in advance, kept a current church calendar, and provided support to committee chairs within the church. He was a faithful pastoral visitor and put a lot of time into preparation for sermons and Sunday worship. The primary difference between the two pastors was that the first one loved being with people and the second one seemed to not want to be with people. He preferred to work in his office, seemed ill at ease when meeting people (even parishioners) outside of the church, and did not have the charisma of the first pastor.

Both pastors had obvious strengths and talents. Both were faithful to their ordination to Word, Sacrament, and Order. Both did their best to be effective pastors and model commitment to Jesus Christ. Only the first one, however, was able to convey a depth of love and concern for his parishioners. His ministry received more affirmation and support than did the second minister's, even though the second minister's standards for his work were higher. Because the people did not know that he loved them, they did not receive what he had to offer them. In a much shorter time than he originally anticipated he left the church.

The example of these two pastors points to the importance of the relationship between pastor and people. If you want to be effective in ministry, you need to be able to relate well with people of all ages. You need to be able to foster authentic and healthy relationships with your people, establish and respect appropriate boundaries, and operate from within an accepted pastoral ethic. When conflict comes—and it will—you will need to understand the dynamics of it and be mature enough to look behind what is being done and said to the underlying pain and fear. You will need to be able to put your own frustrations and hurts aside in order to offer reconciling leadership and lead the way to forgiveness and compromise when it is called for. Through it all, you will need to be able to convey love for your people. If you do not they will not listen to you.

Loving people is not just one more thing on the job description of the pastor. Loving others is only possible if you love yourself. If you do not love yourself, then you are at risk for codependent relationships that cripple ministry and the lives of those involved. When you do love yourself, you are free to love others; the love comes easily and genuinely and is conveyed as such to others. This self-love comes when you know you are loved by God and by others. There is no shortcut to it, and people who have been deprived of love as children often have difficult times establishing loving and mutual relationships as adults.

Your field education experience gives you the opportunity to think about the quality of your relationships with others of all ages. How do you relate to the youngest children in the church? Are you comfortable around them? Do you know what to say to them? Perhaps you will be able to do some children's sermons while you are in the setting. Be sure to seek feedback from your teaching committee about them if you do.

How do you relate with youth? Do you take time to listen to their concerns, whether or not you work directly with the youth group? Do you know what music they like? what movies they are seeing? what their favorite foods are? who their heroes are? Or are you nervous around them and feel like you do not know what to say or how to relate? How do you think they feel about you? What would they say if someone asked them how you felt about them?

What is it like for you to be with adults? Are you most comfortable with your contemporaries or with other generations? I once knew a pastor who was comfortable with young children and the elderly members of the members of church. With the youngest he related like a father; with the oldest he related like a son. Unfortunately the majority of the members of the church were his contemporaries. With that group he was usually ill at ease and conveyed a discomfort and uncertainty that resulted in their concluding that he did not like them.

Have you had any experience relating to the elderly people in your community? Some seminarians naturally gravitate to the older members of their congregations, feel comfortable with them, and are able to establish mutually rewarding relationships with them. Other students shy away from people in the golden years because they do not know what to talk about with them. Sometimes, I suspect, these students have fallen prey to the values of our society that say that the older members of our society and church are not valuable anymore; they have retired from work and from life and have nothing more to offer. At other times, students shy away from the elderly because they view them as being too close to death. I hope you will take the opportunity in your ministry setting to get to know the elderly members of the congregation well. They are the living history of the church and because they are, they shape the future.

Think about the quality of your relationships with others in the field education setting as the year goes on. You may already realize that the church is one of the few places in society where we enjoy intergenerational events each week. Here you may relate to the infant and the ninety-year-old within one morning. As you grow in your trust of your mentor/supervisor, you might discuss those relationships with him or her. Look at them through the lens of love to see what they reveal about your ability to convey warm personal regard and loving intentions to others. See whether they are sufficiently healthy and appropriately mutual. Pray about them, and relate them to your own relationship with God and with yourself. Use the feedback from your committee as data for your consideration for the future. Allow the experience to shape your course work on campus, your conversations with your adviser, and your decisions about counseling or CPE. Any effort you put into improving the quality of your loving relationships with others in ministry will be rewarded beyond measure.

THEOLOGICAL REFLECTION

One of the most important and far-reaching goals of any well constructed field education program is helping students become theologians. Most students do not view themselves as theologians when they enter seminary. If asked to name a theologian, they might name James Cone or Catherine Keller or Karl Barth. It is the exceptional student who realizes early on that he or she is also a theologian. That student knows the question is not, Am I a theologian? but What kind of theologian am I? Am I informed and well read enough to be a thoughtful, articulate, insightful theologian?

In order to be an effective pastoral leader who is responsive to and responsible for the spiritual lives of your congregants you will need to be able to understand issues, situations, comments, and relationships in theological terms. You will need to be able to translate the common into the uncommon, inviting others to see as you do that God is everywhere and in everything.

In many ways, becoming a theologian is like learning a new language. Although it may involve at times words that have a particular meaning in the church, like sanctification and justification, more often than not you will be using your normal everyday language as you "do theology." What makes your reflection theological is that you are translating your ideas and experiences into what I call "God language," that is, you are discovering what God has to do with the daily situations about which you are concerned. The language you use as a theologian is really God's language, language that has taken God into account and addressed the question, What does God have to say about this?

If you have not knowingly done theological reflection before, you may wonder where on earth (or heaven!) to begin. I say *knowingly* because in reality whenever you have attempted to apply the tradition of the faith, the message of the gospel, or your own personal beliefs to life, you have done theological reflection even if you have not understood it in those terms.

One of the most helpful models for doing theological reflection comes from the Wesleyan heritage of the quadrilateral. John Wesley, the founder of Methodism, understood that there are four lenses through which to understand God's will in a given situation in life. These four ways are scripture, tradition, experience, and reason. Wesley believed that by appealing to these four sources, we would come to discern the will of God. They are gifts from God that inform not only our belief but also our practice.

The method we use in Drew's program is one example of a way to think theologically. Students are asked to present situations from their current ministry settings as the basis for the reflection. Such a situation might be a conversation they had when visiting a person in crisis, a meeting they chaired or attended, a program they planned that went well or did not go well. As they soon see, theological reflection can and should be done on any situation or occurrence in life. Remember that the goal of such a disciplined approach is to enable you to increasingly see the world with new eyes, namely, theological eyes.

Once a given student tells the class about the facts of the case, he or she is then invited to become a listener-observer while the rest of the class shares its ideas and moves through the quadrilateral. For example, one day in class a student reported that her church had been asked to sponsor the new senior citizen housing being built in town. The members of the congregation were not certain they wanted to take on the responsibility of such sponsorship even though it would not involve any financial obligation. Following her description of the current situation, the class brought the resources of the quadrilateral to bear on the case study and helped the student to see it in theological terms.

As they explored scripture they saw that there is clear guidance about the relationship of children to their parents, the young to the elderly. Put simply, they saw that children are repeatedly directed to care for their parents and that such care is a way of honoring them. (See Exodus 20:12; Matthew 15:4; and 1 Timothy 5:4, 8.)

Following the exploration of the sacred texts the class moved to examine the tradition of the faith in the early church and throughout history. They saw that the church's practice has been consistent with scripture at many points. The church has been active in caring for the elderly, infirm, and dying throughout the ages. The first hospices were established by the church in the Middle Ages to care for travelers during the Crusades, and many modern hospitals were founded and funded by the church. Many faith communities today are involved in programs designed to care for the homeless or build low income housing through Habitat for Humanity.

Moving to the third part of the quadrilateral, the group spent time talking about the experience of the intergenerational nature of the church. They saw that it is one of the few places in this society where people of all ages regularly meet to have fellowship, work together on programs, learn from each other, and worship freely together. They talked about appreciating the older generation's wisdom, commitment, role modeling, and sense of humor. Through the discussion they affirmed the importance of continuing to support senior citizens not only to maintain the record of scripture and tradition but because the church and community would benefit so much from continued relationship with them. At the same time, they acknowledged that the mobile nature of our society has resulted in dramatic changes in family living situations. Our mobile society, in which families are scattered around the country, has brought with it an increased need for the kind of senior citizen housing under discussion. With societal change, in other words, has come an opportunity for a new and necessary outreach on the part of the church into the community.

Finally the students moved to the fourth part of the quadrilateral, reason. This part of the discussion serves to pull all of the previous reflections together and point the way to some direction and action. The faculty leader asked the students to think about the theological issues raised in the example they were considering. They listed the following:

- care of the elderly and society's views of the aging process
- the need for intergenerational relationships in the church and the world
- stewardship of the church's financial resources
- what it means to represent Christ in the world

The students saw clearly that the record of scripture, the tradition of the church, and their experience of the benefits of the intergenerational nature of the church were lined up together and all pointed in the same direction—namely, in favor of the local congregation sponsoring the senior citizen housing. The student making the initial presentation was better able to go back to her church armed with an appropriate interpretation out of the Christian heritage in favor of sponsoring the senior citizen housing project. Theological reflection had helped her to become clear about the direction the church needed to take. She felt stronger in her conviction about the appropriateness of that direction because it was clearly supported by the mission of the church.

The process of theological reflection involves the study of the covenant relationship between God and God's people through the exploration of scripture and the history of the church. The results of that study are placed alongside contemporary experience and a reasoned approach to the issues being addressed. All of this results in a more clearly delineated course of action called for on the part of the ones engaged in theological reflection.

This method, or one like it, is a crucial tool for pastoral leaders to have. If you are not skilled in helping your people understand the theological dimensions of issues that confront them daily, you will not be able to help them make connections between their lives and the gospel of Jesus Christ. You must be able to lead the way in thinking theologically so that you are able to teach them how to do the same in their own lives. Without this ability, the church will finally fail in its mission because it will cease to be able to apply the witness of the church to the rest of the world. Put another way, Sunday morning will cease to have any influence on Monday morning, or any other time of the week, and society will continue to become more and more secularized with the church becoming more and more marginalized.

PASTORAL IDENTITY AND VOCATIONAL DISCERNMENT

One of the special opportunities of being in a field setting and working closely with a mentor/supervisor is the transformation in one's self-understanding that inevitably results from the process. In every profession the transformation must take place in order for the student to successfully function at higher levels of responsibility. Student teachers, for example, must be able to establish themselves as the authority in the classroom and to command the respect due them as the teacher of the class. Although the children in the classroom may view the student teacher as an accomplished professional, it is the rare student that feels confident in that role to begin with. This is true in every profession, ministry included.

Donald Light has written a book that sheds light on the process of transformation for all students seeking to become established as professionals. In the book *Becoming Psychiatrists: The Professional Transformation of Self,* he provides us with a road map that is useful for understanding ministerial students as well as the residents in psychiatry about whom he is particularly concerned.

Coming to their residency in psychiatry from four years of medical school and having achieved a level of proficiency and self-confidence that befits the hard work and countless hours spent to reach that point, psychiatric residents are surprised and at times alarmed to discover that they are once again neophytes, this time in their chosen professional world. Over the course of the three-year residency they experience predictable challenges and assaults to their self-esteem. Light refers to this process as their moral career.[1]

Light points out that we do not usually think about the moral career of trainees. Nevertheless, the moral career of the resident is as real as the professional career. The ways they make decisions, the values they use, the progress and backsliding along the way are important elements of the resident's professional development and his or her transformation from resident to psychiatrist.

The predictable stops along the way in this journey of transformation are the following:

1. Feeling different and being discredited
2. Moral confusion

3. Numbness and exhaustion
4. Moral transition
5. Self-affirmation[2]

For much of the first year residents feel inadequate and as if they have no real contribution to make in the care of their patients. They become uncertain about how to make a diagnosis, begin to doubt their own abilities, and wonder if they chose the right specialty in medicine.

As the program goes into the second year and they continue to work long hours, they experience an exhaustion and numbness that presents them with a crossroads of sorts. They must face the inevitable and important decision: to continue or to quit. It is a time in which the resident must call upon all of his or her spiritual and emotional resources and answer the question: Who am I? with conviction and a fair amount of certainty. Answering this important question marks the moral transition of the resident. Those who remain in the program go on to increased confidence and clear direction in their professional development.

Though a lengthy and arduous process to be sure, the professional formation of the resident is an important one. Without such a three-year period, the resident would not become a professional in the deepest sense of the word. She would remain dependent upon authority figures for diagnoses and direction and would be incapable of rendering quality psychiatric care.

Seminary students have a similar journey ahead of them as they move through the curriculum and engage in the practice of ministry at the same time. Although some students come to seminary with years of experience in ministry, most do not. Most come with some ideas about what is involved in ministerial leadership but never have served in that role. While their experience as church members and leaders is helpful in that it gives them a knowledge of church culture, it does not of course give them the knowledge of what it feels like to assume the responsibility of pastoral leadership. That is something that comes only with lived experience.

Field education will provide you with the opportunity to try on the office of pastoral leader surrounded by a safety net of support, affirmation, and direction offered by your mentor/supervisor and laity. Like the psychiatric resident, you must go through a formation process that will result either in your claiming your pastoral identity or deciding that another vocational direction is more appropriate.

The stages Dr. Light outlines for psychiatric residents provide a useful description of the process for seminary students in field education. I have often heard students talk about feeling different and confused early on in the field education process. Many students have commented on how disconcerting it was to put the pulpit robe on for the first time and how startled they were to realize that when parishioners said "Hello, Reverend" they were addressing them! Confusion about whether, how, when, and what to pray abounds during the year in field education. Many report feeling humbled and frightened by the obvious high expectations parishioners have for the student's wisdom and ability to solve long-standing problems that have plagued the church.

While they feel confused students also report feeling tired and even exhausted. This tiredness is partially a result of the multiple demands upon the time and energy of students in graduate school. But it cannot be laid at the door of their schedule entirely. It takes an enormous amount of energy to change one's self-understanding and inner identity. It is hard work to go from viewing oneself as a layperson to a professional in any field. It is perhaps harder for those who seek ordination because of the magnitude of the responsibility they will be assuming.

The questions facing you in seminary are the largest questions humankind ever faces: Why are we here? What is the meaning of life? Who is God? Why is there suffering? How can we account for the evil in the world? What does justice look like? What happens after we die? The care of souls is an extremely important work with effects that last for eternity. You will find not only that you must wrestle with the answers to these questions for yourself but that you must also be prepared to help others wrestle with them. This is a difficult task sometimes, made more difficult because you realize the extent to which others are counting on your wisdom and insight and "connection" to God for their direction. Put simply, you will find that sometimes others will expect more of you than you think you are capable of giving. Especially in the early stages of your pastoral formation this knowledge can be a heavy, albeit welcomed, burden to bear.

As time goes on and you continue to reflect on your ministry through the field education program, you will begin to realize that you feel differently inside. You have begun the moral transition from layperson to pastoral leader. Unless you have decided at some point that you do not want to seek ordination, you will feel more and more like a pastor and will operate from within that framework of self-understanding. When you ask yourself the question, Who am I? your answer will come more quickly and with greater conviction: I am a pastor. You will feel more confident as you perform the duties of the office, more comfortable with others' acceptance of you as "Reverend," and more at ease wrestling with the hard questions of life. In short, the process of pastoral formation, coming as it does through a time of testing and reflection, is a necessary one if you want to continue down the road to ordination and effective pastoral leadership in the years to come.

SPIRITUAL GROWTH

Spiritual growth undergirds all else; without it your ministry will finally fail. You will find that while you are in seminary you will be challenged daily on a spiritual level. Each day you will be confronted with new ways of thinking about God and humanity, new ways of reading and understanding scripture, new ways of thinking about yourself and your ultimate values. As the semesters unfold you will be exposed to multiple ways of worship, different faith commitments and formulations, and diverse views on subjects ranging from the nature of sin to the proper understanding of the funeral rites of the church.

All of these things will push you to examine and reexamine what *you* yourself believe about the Triune God we know in Jesus Christ. Hopefully you will have ample opportunities to worship with your seminary community during each week and will be exposed to different liturgical forms and styles of sermons. All of these things will push you to look at your own faith commitments with new eyes. I have spoken elsewhere of the challenge of renegotiating one's faith in light of the academic experience. This challenge is usually felt keenly and results in changes in the spirituality of students who are honest with themselves and open to the experience.

The changes take different forms, to be sure. Some students' eyes are opened in new ways to social justice issues and their relationship to the gospel. They understand ministry and their call from God in a different way because of this and begin to think more carefully about leadership and its challenges and opportunities.

Some students become more eager and comfortable witnessing to their own faith in Christ, having opportunities to do so in many places in seminary. Others become aware that theirs is a private faith and must struggle with finding appropriate and comfortable ways to share their beliefs with others, knowing that if they do not do that while they are in seminary, they will have difficulty doing it in ministry beyond seminary.

Some students become more intentional about the practice of the spiritual disciplines (prayer, Bible study, private and corporate worship, fasting) while others become less disciplined. Some students come to the realization that their spiritual lives are fed by many different things: their intellect, their relationships, their emotions, their bodies. This realization is an expansion of their previously held notion that the only real way to be fed spiritually is in church on Sunday morning. A change that often accompanies this realization is that students begin to move from a highly individualized spirituality to a more communally based spirituality.

I will speak about more of these changes in a subsequent chapter. Suffice it to note here that your spiritual life is no different from the other areas affected through the field education experience. This challenge to your spirituality is good because it is usually the occasion for a deepening of one's roots in God and a greater sophistication in one's understanding of the realm of the Unseen. As Paul says,

> We also boast in our sufferings, knowing that suffering produces endurance, and endurance produces character, and character produces hope, and hope does not disappoint us, because God's love has been poured into our hearts through the Holy Spirit that has been given to us. (Romans 5:3-5)

The congregation among whom you minister will need to know that you are a man or woman for whom faith in God through Christ is central. If you have not taken advantage of the rich resources and opportunities for reflection and growth in both seminary and your field education program and therefore have not grown spiritually, it means that you are closed-spirited. To be closed in one's spirit means that you are closed to God and to God's activity in your life and in the lives of others around you.

I hope you will take some time while you are in field education to discuss with your mentor/supervisor how he or she maintains a lively spiritual life, how it relates to ongoing ministry, and how it relates to his or her leadership in the particular setting. A related concern is how the supervisor promotes opportunities for spiritual growth among the congregation on a regular basis. I hope you will also discuss these issues with your lay committee. If you do your ideas about the nature of spirituality will be enriched and expanded. That is all to the good, for any effective pastoral leader knows that there are as many expressions of spirituality as there are people in the world. The competent pastoral-spiritual leader is able to understand and relate these differing expressions as they present themselves.

EXPERIENTIAL LEARNING

It is not always easy to manage the responsibilities that come through the field education experience on top of the other demands upon students' time. Drew Theological School, for example, requires students to be in ministry at least twelve to fifteen hours per week. Some of this time may be spent in preparation as needed; however, the clear majority of the time is spent in the field education setting itself. In addition to these hours, some students commute distances to their ministry settings once or twice a week, depending upon the situation and the program that week. Students have varying reactions to these weekly time demands.

Some students are eager to be in ministry through the field education program. They feel more alive, more energized, more completely themselves during the time they are in ministry each week.

Their experience tends to reinforce the excitement of holding the pastoral office, and while they become more and more aware of the challenges and difficulties of ministry, they are not over-whelmed by them. Instead, they view them as opportunities to further spread the gospel and offer influential leadership as a pastoral person.

This enthusiasm for the practice of ministry is laudable as long as it is balanced in equal parts with a love of learning in the academy. I recall a student who had a wonderful experience in her field education site. Her supervisor was supportive and encouraging, challenged her to grow in many ways, expected her to function at a high level, and encouraged her to become involved in as many areas of ministry as she was inclined. She enjoyed being in the church and felt affirmed whenever she was there. While it was a positive experience in some ways, she allowed her church work to overshadow her studies as the semester wore on.

The truth of the matter was that she loved being in her church because she was receiving a lot of affirmation for the work she was doing there. In contrast to that affirmation, she felt inadequate as a seminary student. She was taking some challenging classes that required her to master difficult material and to read hundreds of pages each week. Added to that challenge were some personal self-esteem issues from her past that were causing her to feel as if she would never amount to much no matter what she did. This student judged that she needed affirmation and needed it now. Her church assignment was the place she was receiving that affir-mation, not the seminary. Therefore she decided to spend as much time in the church as she could, even if it meant shortchanging her seminary experience and work.

Unfortunately, she did shortchange her seminary experience, and herself in the process. The months she neglected to attend class and participate in classroom discussions, the after-hours dor-mitory discussions she missed that allow students to continue to wrestle with issues raised in class, and the chance to absorb more of the spiritual nurture through chapel and community life were all missing for her and could never be regained.

This student serves as an example of someone who is pulled too much in the direction of field education. Other students have different reactions to this part of the required curriculum. One of the most common reactions comes from students who are second career students.

Some students have held very responsible positions in the work force. Such a background can significantly color their view of being in supervised positions. One student came to seminary at age 57, having been a vice president of a major oil corporation. He had clearly demonstrated leadership abilities before arriving at seminary.

He came at ministry with the same high energy, enthusiasm, and belief in himself that had been present in his work in the corporate world. Although he was eager to be in a church setting, however, he balked at the notion that he needed to be supervised while he did it. He expected the same level of autonomy when he was in a church. Although his self-confidence was a decided asset, it also had a negative aspect to it. He failed to understand that although he was a seasoned corporate leader, he was in fact a novice in terms of pastoral leadership in a church setting. It took some time for him to comprehend that his needing supervision in that setting did not diminish his value or capabilities in anyone's eyes. The experience was a humbling one for him, and it contributed to his spiritual growth as he moved from arrogance to humility.

I have seen another reaction to field education, one that blocks students from learning all they can from the experience. This reaction comes from students who have grown up in the church and held many different leadership positions across the years. A similar reaction has sometimes come from students who have served as pastors before they come to seminary. Some of these students have told me that they do not need to take the required course in supervised ministry because of their prior and current experience in the church. In other words, they believe that they know the church and the pastoral office well enough to not need any further time of reflection or study on the subject.

Such students often try to make the case that they need other courses more than field education and point out that if they are exempted from field education they will be able to take more elective courses and pursue advanced study. Whenever such a student talks to me in this way, I am quick to point out that their argument, if carried to its logical conclusion, means that they do not necessarily need to take any required courses. For example, they might argue that because they have read the Bible all of their lives they do not need to take any courses in biblical studies. Likewise, because they have heard many sermons in their lifetime they do not need to study the structure or form of the sermon, or spend any time reflecting on the goals of the sermon or its location within a worship service and setting. I usually conclude my remarks by saying that their wanting to be excused from field education because they are familiar with the church is akin to the hypochondriac who says she does not need to go to medical school to practice medicine because she has spent so much time with doctors, having been sick so much of her life!

Finally, I have heard students over the years make disparaging remarks about the field education enterprise as a required program. While clearly in the minority, these students view field education as somehow irrelevant or not as academically respectable as other courses in seminary. When I have talked with my colleagues in field education at other institutions, I have heard similar stories about students who dismiss field education as a worthwhile enterprise.

Field education will be a demanding time for you in terms of both time management and general challenges to your spiritual and professional growth. You will be pushed to think more creatively and in a more sophisticated way about the nature of ministry and yourself as a ministering person, as well as the nature of the church and its place in the twenty-first century.

You Received Without Payment . . .

At the start of this chapter I referred to a conversation I had with a friend at college about despairing of ever finishing school and being in full-time ministry. He wisely invited me to reframe my entire view of ministry and helped me see it in a different light.

Before my conversation with him I thought of ministry as something that could only take place in the future. Obviously I was not yet ready to minister to others: I had to finish college and then attend three more years of seminary. Underlying this view of ministry was the idea that only those with sufficient education and preparation could rightfully be called ministers. Ministry, according to that definition, was a set of ideas to be shared, sermons to be preached, prayers to be offered. It was what an ordained person did to and for and with other persons only after that ordained person had enough education and experience to be ordained.

Dale changed all that by helping me to reframe my understanding of ministry. First he challenged the notion that I had to be a particular age to be a minister. At the time of our conversation I was 19 years old. I had only known ministers who were much older (in their 30s, for example!) and who had long since finished their formal education. Dale challenged that idea by saying that I could be a minister right at that moment. What needed changing was not my age but my attitude.

Next Dale's words challenged the clericalism that lurked within my unexamined views of the nature of ministry. It had never occurred to me to look at myself or any other layperson as a minister or to think that I could be in ministry anywhere, anytime. How new and wonderful an idea that was to me!

This freedom to minister anywhere, anytime, anyhow is seen in the sending forth of the apostles by Jesus Christ in Matthew 10. It is clear from these verses that the disciples are "traveling light." They are not concerned about their next meal or where they will spend the night. They are not worrying about receiving a salary or whether someone likes them or not. They simply take the power of God through Christ, which they have received freely, and give it freely to others wherever they find themselves among the people of Israel. The ministry Jesus asks them to perform is not something that can only happen after they have sufficiently studied, are sufficiently old, or are sufficiently wise at some future point in time. Ministry happens now, for they have received what they need—namely, power from God.

Each fall I start the supervised ministry seminar by inviting students and faculty to join me in the chapel for the last half hour of class on the first day it meets. During a brief service we celebrate the ministry our students will be offering the world through the year and recognize their work liturgically. During the service they are asked to commit themselves to doing their best to bring Christ to the people and situations they will encounter during the coming year. This affirms the value of what they will be doing and supports them as students continuing to learn what it means to offer pastoral leadership in a hurting and broken world.

I say the same to you: though you may not yet be ordained, you are still able to be in ministry. Through the resources of your seminary program and community, your ministry will be developed and strengthened, and you will be blessed in countless ways in the process.

EXERCISE

Take some time to think about what you hope to learn through the field education program at your seminary. What do you need to learn in the area of pastoral skills? What do you need to work on in terms of your personality or style of relating with others?

How would you assess your spiritual life as you read this book? Do you feel close to God today or far away? What is your prayer life like now? Is it stronger and deeper than it was before you came to seminary or more shallow? Why?

Think more about your call to ministry. How can you use your field education experience to help you discern with greater clarity and conviction what God wants you to do in ministry? Do you believe God is calling you to be ordained or to some other kind of ministry?

When you have thought about all of these things, take some time for prayer and meditation. Invite God into your hopes and expectations and goals for your field education experience. Ask God to guide you through the process and help you to discover the gifts for ministry you have been given, refine your understanding of what ministry is and is not, and come to clearer knowledge of the direction God is calling you to go. Give thanks for all that will be revealed to you through the field education process, and ask God's blessing upon you and those with whom you will be in covenant relationship.

Prayer: Gracious God, be my teacher throughout my time in field education. Help me to view the experience as a vineyard that belongs to you. Give me encouragement, stamina, courage, enthusiasm, grace, and love for all I meet. Enable me to hear in the feedback I receive through the year your dear voice calling me to particular ministry in the world. Bless my supervisor, lay committee, professors, and fellow students, who are all trying to help me hear your call more clearly in my own life through this process. Help me to remain open to the reflection, discussion, and evaluation that are at the heart of the field education program. Draw me closer to yourself that I may become more like you every day. In the name of Christ I pray. Amen.

CHAPTER 7

Money and Time Management

Consider the lilies of the field, how they grow; they neither toil nor spin, yet I tell you, even Solomon in all his glory was not clothed like one of these. Matthew 6:28-29

I planted, Apollos watered, but God gave the growth.

1 Corinthians 3:6

n this chapter I address two issues that are related to the quality of your ministry over the years: time and money. If you are ordained, your vocation will be service to others in the name of Jesus Christ. The hours will be long, and the pay will usually be relatively small. You will be expected to be available around the clock and to be content with your small salary and the house that will probably accompany it. You may be in situations in which little regard is paid for your day off and your church(es) does not have the financial resources to increase your salary.

Because of the nature and role of the pastoral office in the community of faith, you will need to be able to establish healthy boundaries for yourself. You will need to be able to take charge of your time and your schedule and not be pulled in several different directions at once. Working with your people you will need to establish goals for yourself and the ministry of the church that are reachable and realistic and organize your time and efforts accordingly.

You will also need to know how to learn to live within a budget. In The United Methodist Church, candidates for ordination are asked the historic questions used since John Wesley founded the church in the eighteenth century. One of the questions, "Are you in debt so as to embarrass you in your work?"[1] is a difficult one for some candidates to answer honestly. Wesley understood that carrying a debt can be debilitating to ministers because it brings added stress and may cause clergy to look outside the ministry for additional sources of income.

It is a rare person entering ministry who has no debt whatsoever. The spirit of Wesley's question should not suggest that ordinands should not owe a penny to anyone, but rather that they should not be so weighed down by a burden of debt that they cannot function in ministry with its low salary. I am glad this question is asked of candidates because it serves as reminder to them that the quality of our finances is related to the quality of our ministry. *discuss* A similar question might be asked of seminarians who need to learn the same lesson.

Issues of money and time management will come to the fore fairly early in your seminary career. You will probably receive a bill for your first semester even before classes begin. Once you have finished your first week of classes, you will realize that each minute must be put to good use if you are to stay on top of the classwork required each week. If you do not, you will very quickly fall behind in your reading and writing and find it difficult to catch up.

When I began college I naively thought that since my brother and sister were in college at the same time my family would be eligible for scholarships and loans. I was surprised to discover that because both of my parents worked we were ineligible for need-based assistance. The formula used to assess financial need indicated that we did not have any need, even though my parents were paying three tuition bills each semester.

As I began my sophomore year I made an appointment to see the vice president of the college. After I told him that in order to remain in school I would need more scholarship aid, he offered me a job on campus in the print shop. I began working between fifteen and twenty hours per week. The money I earned allowed me to pay for my books and incidental expenses for the remainder of the time I was in college.

That job was to serve me well beyond college. By the time I entered seminary my mother was a widow. She was still teaching and able to support herself, but not able to assist me with the costs of theological education. I knew upon arriving at seminary that I would need to work in order to pay the bills.

During the orientation program I located the print shop on campus and went to see the woman who was the head of the department. When I told her that I knew how to run all of the machines in the office and asked for a job, she hired me on the spot. I once again spent from fifteen to twenty hours per week working while I was in school. I also got a job working in a church when the semester began and continued to do both until I graduated three years later.

I was grateful for the opportunity to pay for my theological education without taking out more government loans. As it was, I was carrying several thousand dollars of debt on my college education, which I was responsible for paying. It was not always easy to juggle the time demands of two jobs in addition to a full load of classes, but I was grateful to be able to pay my own way without turning to my mother or the government.

The costs of higher education have soared, as have general living costs. For example, my tuition bill for a year of college was $2,400 in 1968. Tuition for an academic year at the same institution now costs $19,000. Theological schools vary in the amount of tuition they charge. According to the ATS research office, the range of tuition rates in theological schools today goes from $0 to nearly $19,000 per academic year. The average yearly tuition and fees for the Master of Divinity degree during the 1996-97 academic year in all ATS member schools was between $4,709 and $5,062.[2] That represents an average increase in tuition and fees over the previous year of 4.1 percent.[3]

Billing offices usually assume students will be full time and bill accordingly. If you decide to change the number of credit hours you take during a given semester, your bill will be changed accordingly and your financial aid will be adjusted as well. You should maintain the same percentage of assistance with a different dollar amount credited to your account.

You school's financial assistance office may be able to give you a figure that helps you prepare your own personal budget for the coming year. For example, Drew's office estimates the expense for a single, full-time student living on campus to be $20,030. Married students will, of course, need to budget more because apartment living on campus is more expensive than sharing a room in a dormitory. Food costs will obviously be more for families than for single students.

Unless your seminary is one that does not charge tuition, you can expect your costs each year to be sizable. I have talked with many perspective students over the years who expressed a great desire to attend seminary but were intimidated by what they viewed as the out-of-reach expenses. Most of those prospective students turned into matriculated students sooner or later; they found a way to pay the bills—so will you.

Another issue facing some seminary students is debt acquired prior to matriculating in a program of graduate theological education. A study done by the Auburn Center for the Study of Theological Education between 1990 and 1994 shows that 5 percent of students graduating from theological and rabbinical schools in 1991 brought undergraduate debt of $10,000 to their graduate programs. Ten percent brought undergraduate debt of $7500. Although the vast majority of students (nearly 65 percent) did not report any undergraduate debt, a few who reported it were carrying a burdensome level into a vocation that for the most part does not pay well. The Auburn study also revealed the following:

> Those students who bring undergraduate educational debt with them are highly likely to add to that debt in theological school: of these, eighty-eight percent of Master of Divinity graduates and eighty-four percent of two-year masters degree graduates borrow additional amounts while in theological school.[4]

Clearly it is better not to carry heavy levels of debt upon graduation. Most mainline Protestant denominations pay salaries well below those of comparable secular positions. Most pastors can expect to be earning considerably less than at least some of their parishioners, especially if those parishioners are professionals. The strategies outlined below will enable you to stay in seminary with your head above financial water. Above all, I hope you will make yourself a promise that you will do all within your power, including taking a leave of absence in order to work for a semester or year if it proves necessary, to graduate with minimal debt.

PAYING THE BILLS

You need to check with your financial aid office if you have not already done so to see what assistance the school may give you when you are a matriculated student. Financial assistance (also called financial aid) is awarded two ways: through demonstrated merit or need. Merit-based scholarships are awarded to people who show unusual academic or personal promise. In the case of theological schools, merit-based moneys are given to students who exhibit particularly strong academic records from prior work, have outstanding references that highlight their suitability for ministry, or have written personal statements of particularly high quality.

When a school is awarding federal moneys to students based on need, its awarding process will be determined by federal regulations. If you are attending such a school, a set formula will be used to ascertain whether or not you demonstrate need. If you do, it will be determined at what level, and the dollar amount will be fixed accordingly.

School scholarships are only one source of funding, however. Many churches or church bodies, foundations, and individuals have assisted theological students. Talk with a counselor in your school's financial aid office for some suggestions as to where you might apply for funding in addition to that awarded by the school. I also recommend checking with your dean's office to inquire about additional outside scholarship sources.

You may also finance your theological degree by taking out loans, either through a government loan program or your local bank. There are currently two government loan programs available to you: Perkins and Stafford. These programs offer relatively low interest rates. The Perkins program lends money at a rate of 5 percent while the Stafford rate varies but has 8.25 percent as a cap. There is usually a grace period of six to eight months after graduation before you begin paying back the loans.

A third way you may be able to finance your theological education is through the federal *work study* program. This program allows eligible students to earn a predesignated amount by working a certain number of hours per week. Work study jobs are usually on campus; occasionally they are off-campus. One thing all work study jobs have in common is that they do not involve any religious work whatsoever. Your financial aid officer will inform you if you are eligible for work study, which depends upon your income level and assets.

In addition to work study, loans, and scholarship aid, many students work one or two jobs in order to pay for school and living expenses. If you were to poll your fellow students, you would probably find that the vast majority of them are working at least one job while attending school.

The Auburn study on theological students' debt found that most Protestant students work over ten hours per week while in their final year of seminary, with significant numbers working over twenty hours. The following bar graph displays the data from that study by the denomination of the student respondents.

It is beyond the scope of this book to analyze the above data extensively or to raise questions about denominational support for seminarians. I simply invite you to compare your experience with that of your colleagues in school and in the denomination. I also urge you to talk with your denominational officials to ensure that you have explored all avenues of support from that source. My experience has been that in too many cases money was available at the denominational level for students who did not know about it and therefore did not apply for it.

The experience of working while being in seminary is often a difficult one, but it can be done. Many students continue to work full time while attending seminary and find a way to juggle multiple demands upon their time. They often take evening or summer classes in order to be able to make sufficient academic progress and finish their Master of Divinity degree within three years while continuing to work full time the entire three years. Although it is not easy, they are motivated to continue studying year-round and need the income their job provides. Usually these students do well academically; they are highly organized in addition to being motivated, learn all they can, and graduate on time.

Most students I know work part time instead of full time. They are able to afford to go to school because of the financial aid package they receive and the outside funds they have in addition. Married students may or may not need to work while in seminary. Sometimes spouses work full time, which allows the student to not work an additional job beyond what is required for supervised ministry. Students who have children may, however, need to work because the financial needs of the family dictate it.

Hours of Work Per Week for Pay in Final Year – Proportions of Master of Divinity Graduates, by Denomination of Student. Denominations with Twenty or More Respondents.[5]

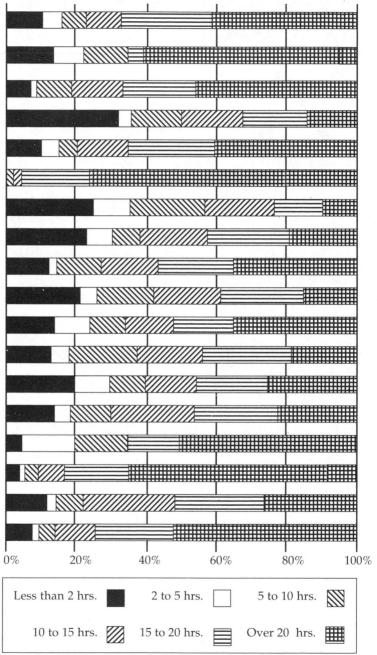

Less than 2 hrs. 2 to 5 hrs. 5 to 10 hrs. 10 to 15 hrs. 15 to 20 hrs. Over 20 hrs.

Anyone in ministry today needs to be a good manager of personal finances and church finances. The realities of full-time Christian service are such that you should not expect to earn a large salary at any point in your active years of ministry. You would do well to prepare yourself for that reality by starting in seminary to live on a budget. Calculate your expenses and income for the month and the year. Draw up a plan that will allow you to pay your bills on time and, if possible, to save even a modest amount.

CLERGY AND MONEY

There is in many circles the assumption that clergy are not capable of handling finances or thinking about money matters in an informed and sophisticated way. Clergy, so the popular view goes, spend all their time thinking about spiritual matters (and so they should) and think nothing about things of the material world (and so they should not). If the goal of the clergy is to lead their congregations to heaven, it follows that they could not and would not, therefore, be very adept at the ways of the world, especially money matters.

The view extends in many cases to the point at which some church members are appalled when their pastor asks for a raise—pastors are not supposed to care about money in the least. If a pastor does ask for a raise, that is proof that the pastor's heart is not in the ministry and that he or she is too much concerned with the material world for the congregation's own good!

In fairness to this view, let me point out that behind it is a desire for clergy to be as Jesus was: in the world but not of the world. In a society that is at once highly individualized, competitive, and materialistic, clergy are viewed as being immune (or at least they ought to be) to the temptation to care more about acquiring material goods than laying up treasure in heaven.

Although I have some sympathy with this view, I also understand that clergy need to be concerned with keeping body and soul together, earning a reasonable living, supporting their families, educating their children, and providing for their future. As my wise supervisor once put it, "Clergy should not be so heavenly minded that they are no earthly good!"

His wisdom points to the importance of clergy understanding the material stresses and realities of this world, and not only so they can survive themselves. If you do not understand budgets and the pressures of financial obligations, how will you relate to your parishioners who most definitely *do* live with these realities all of the time?

Seminary is a good time to think about issues of how you spend your money. It is also a good time to consider your use of time, for that too is an important consideration in ministry. We will return to considerations of money later in the chapter; we now look at issues of the use of time.

TIME MANAGEMENT

As the rain falls on the just and the unjust alike, so the just and the unjust of the world get the same number of hours per week—168 to be exact. What we do with them determines the quality of our existence, spiritually speaking. We can use them to better ourselves and the world around us, or use them in such a way that we become increasingly stressed and fearful, thereby helping no one else to live more abundantly.

What follow are two examples of the kinds of time demands seminary students are faced with. Example 1 represents a single, full-time student living on campus. Example 2 is a married student with two children, living off campus, and commuting a distance daily.

Example 1		*Example 2*	
14	class hours	14	class hours
28	hours preparation[6]	28	hours preparation
10	hours working	20	hours working
12	hours church work	12	hours church work
21	hours for meals[7]	21	hours for meals
2	hours for laundry	2	hours for laundry
49	hours sleeping	49	hours sleeping
136	hours total	8	hours commuting[8]
		14	hours family time
		168	hours total

You can see that the bulk of the week is very quickly taken up by repetitive and necessary tasks. The single student in example 1 has 32 hours left per week to develop a daily devotional practice, pursue a personal life, go to the movies, visit friends, or read a good novel. The student who is married with children and commuting one hour each way has no time left, however. My experience with these students is that two things begin to be eroded almost immediately, their personal devotional time and their family time.

This exercise is useful because it can open your eyes to why you always feel as if you never have enough time. In my experience it is a rare seminarian who feels there are enough hours in the day. This pressure is particularly felt during exam time and when major papers are due in one or more classes.

The exercise is also useful because seminary serves as an introduction to the world of ministry from the perspective of the required and repetitive tasks of ministry. Look at the example below of a typical pastor's week. Remember that this pastor has the same 168 hours per week that you do! You will see that preparation for Sunday worship and teaching a Bible study are priorities for Pastor Adams, as are pastoral visitation and family time.

Pastor Adams' Week

4	hours personal devotional time (average)[9]
15	hours sermon preparation[10]
2	hours worship/bulletin preparation
2	hours preparation for Bible study
4	hours Sunday morning worship/Sunday school
15	hours pastoral visitation in homes and hospitals
10	hours in church meetings
10	hours general administration
4	hours in community concerns[11]
1	hour in denominational activities[12]
2	hours pastoral counseling
21	hours meals
3	hours church fellowship functions[13]
14	hours family time[14]
2	hours exercise
49	hours sleeping
158	hours total

You can see that Pastor Adams has 10 hours left this week! You will notice that this schedule leaves no time for responding to emergencies in the lives of parishioners and no time for their stopping by the church office to speak with their pastor. "Interruptions" like these in the daily life of a pastor are often the most important parts of ministry. The wise pastor understands this and plans some time for these unexpected occurrences. In other words, do not leave your sermon for Saturday night because you might be spending Saturday night visiting a family in crisis.

The point of this exercise is that the full schedule you have in seminary is not unlike the one you will have in the ministry. You will discover in ministry that there is always more to be done than there are hours in the week. Crises arise with greater or lesser frequency depending upon the week, and the legitimate needs of your parishioners for support, direction, and spiritual guidance never go away. Because you will spend a great deal of time alone, with no one telling you what to do and when to do it, it is imperative that you are able to be focused and organized. Put another way, you will be your own boss. If you cannot be organized and disciplined about the way you spend your time, you will not be able to accomplish the ministry that needs to be done each week in order for your congregation to grow spiritually or otherwise.

The same could be said of seminary. Professors assign readings and papers and exams, but you will be in charge of your schedule, and whether or not you meet deadlines is entirely up to you. If you do not learn how to manage your time in seminary, you will not succeed in learning all you will need to be an effective minister across the years.

If you have never taken a time management workshop, I recommend that you do so. Check with the dean of students or counseling center of your school to see if they offer workshops in things like speed reading, time management, the ordination process, and personal growth groups.

Sometimes students have difficulties with managing their time because of psychological problems. I once knew a student who was routinely late with assignments because he continually procrastinated. He was a perfectionist who was loathe to put his ideas on paper since he knew they would not be good enough. This student had serious psychological problems stemming from having grown up in an alcoholic family in which he felt responsible for his father's drinking. He found it difficult to imagine that he might succeed at anything in life since his father's legacy to him was a deep feeling of inadequacy. This feeling was expressed in his repeatedly putting off assignments. Unfortunately, his was a self-fulfilling prophecy; he thought he would do poorly and therefore put off doing the work, which resulted in lower grades. It was a vicious cycle that needed to be broken by psychological counseling and by his learning some time management techniques. The student entered into a counseling relationship in which he discussed both personal issues and time management. Although seminary remained a struggle for him to a certain degree, he did learn to function at a higher level and turned in his papers on time with greater frequency.

SEMINARY LIFE

In addition to the time demands outlined above, there are other unseen but none the less real elements of seminary life that require time and will affect your week. They have to do with community life and the nature of the subjects you will study. Without repeating what I have said elsewhere, let me remind you that an important part of what you learn in seminary comes from community life. The relationships; the issues; the personal, vocational, and theological questions raised in seminary—all require energy. Being with a community of people striving for similar vocational goals is an enormously rewarding experience, and you will not want to shortchange yourself by returning to your room or leaving campus as soon as class is finished. Do not forget to factor in community fellowship time when you are planning your week—your seminary experience will be the richer for it and therefore your ministry will be as well.

In addition to community time, you will need to find time to exercise each week if you do not already do so. Long hours of study and work will place great demands upon you physically, and regular exercise will help you to stay healthy and in shape.

Current recommendations are 30 minutes, three times a week of some aerobic activity. Walking, running, volleyball, swimming, or some other kind of activity will help you to maintain a good weight and a good energy level, both of which are important in seminary and in ministry. Think of your exercise time as time spent taking care of God's temple, and do not neglect it. You might even incorporate some prayer time into your exercise routine if possible. I often use morning walks as a time when I center myself and pray for myself and for the world. I have found such times to be rich and helpful ones that set the tone for a day in which I am more conscious of God's presence and grace and better able to respond to people and situations with the same grace.

Your changing relationship with God will take time for you to sort out. You will need to develop or continue to have a personal devotional time so that this relationship can grow and provide the foundation for your life and reflections, in seminary now and ministry in the future.

When you reach the point at which you are eligible to apply for ordination, you will need to allow sufficient time for study and writing. Each denomination has its own requirements in terms of written work and historical and theological examinations. Although they vary from church to church, they all require a lot of time and careful thought. You will probably know what will be required of you well before the materials are actually due. If you may pursue ordination while you are in seminary, that will allow you to make some choices about classes with those requirements in mind.

For example, United Methodist students know that they will be asked to respond to the questions in the *Discipline* in addition to writing and teaching a Bible study and preaching at a Sunday worship service. Many students begin looking at those questions at least six months before they are going to be writing their papers. Those who fail to do so find it extremely difficult to insert the production of ordination materials into an already busy semester full of other written work. From a time management perspective, I urge you to be thinking about your ordination requirements well before you are called upon to do any written work.

Such foresight is an important skill in ministry, in any event. Since the church calendar is predictable, the wise pastor thinks at least one season ahead. If, for example, I do not have Lent in mind when I am planning for Advent, how can I ensure that there will be a connection between the two in the minds of my people?

LILIES AND APOLLOS

As I look back over fifteen plus years in theological education, I see two themes repeated over and over again in the conversations I have had with students. These themes have to do with time and money. To summarize them, they are: "I don't have enough money" and "I don't have enough time."

While understandable, these attitudes can promote a mind-set that will be detrimental in your ministry. It makes good sense that you want enough money to pay your bills, care for yourself and your family, be able to give proportionally to the work of the church, and have enough left over to engage in some kind of recreation and enjoyment. It also makes sense that you want to be able to do the work of ministry with a sense of accomplishment that is unhampered by the frustration of always having too much to do in any one day.

The problems come in ministry when a disproportionate amount of your time and energy goes to wanting more money than you have and fretting about work undone. The simple truth is that all of us could use more money and none of us have enough hours in the day. The pastor who becomes consumed with not having enough of either or both will not be able to focus on the work of ministry with integrity and enthusiasm.

I once knew a pastor who was in a church of three hundred members with an average attendance of one hundred. The financial base of the church was not strong, despite its being located in an fairly affluent area. In my conversations with the pastor I was often impressed by the amount of time he spent talking about money—his own. He expected a certain raise the second year he was at the church and was surprised and bitterly disappointed when he did not get it. The reason he did not receive the raise was because the church was losing members and was in serious financial difficulty. Despite the very real difficulties the church was having, the pastor was unable to shift his focus from himself to the health of the congregation.

I knew that the pastor's salary was a good one in comparison to many others. I also knew that his wife worked outside the home and that together they had been able to put their three children through college. At the point in time I am referring to, the pastor did not have greater financial needs than he had when his children were in college. He did, however, have greater ego needs than I wish he had.

His desire for more money was linked to his feeling unappreciated in general and his being needful of more congregational and denominational support. He began to focus more and more on money and on what he viewed as necessary improvements in the parsonage.

As this was going on, or perhaps because it was going on, his enthusiasm for ministry and the quality of his work suffered. He became more self-focused and less other-focused. His people sensed his pulling away from them, and their general dissatisfaction grew.

I tell this story because it illustrates the relationship between our views of money and the quality of our ministry. As Jesus said many years ago, "where your treasure is, there your heart will be also" (Matthew 6:21). This pastor's treasure was found in his paycheck and not in his people or his God. Hence, his heart and mind and energy were spent more and more in consideration of his remuneration. The ministry and the people suffered as a consequence.

You may read this example and respond that perhaps pastors need to think about their own salaries because they usually are low. I respond that while that may be true, worrying about it will not change it one bit. On the contrary, worrying about it and focusing on it may not only hamper your ministry, it may have serious spiritual consequences, for at the heart of such worry is a basic mistrust of God. As you can imagine, mistrust of God is a serious problem for any pastor to grapple with.

Jesus offers a splendid antidote to worry about finances that is at once practical and wise. In the Sermon on the Mount we read the following:

"Consider the lilies of the field, how they grow; they neither toil nor spin, yet I tell you, even Solomon in all his glory was not clothed like one of these." (Matthew 6:28-29)

These beautiful words in Matthew's Gospel are part of a much larger sermon in which Jesus talks about a certain quality of life made possible when one dwells with God. If you have not already done so, I recommend reading the entire Sermon on the Mount in Matthew 5–7. Rather than a life filled with worry and anxiety, hardness of heart and absence of love and loving relationships, Jesus speaks of a life of joy and reconciliation and peace. Rather than a life that is hopeless and empty, Jesus offers a life that is rich with love and free from alarm because it is lived within the Kingdom of Heaven that is even now present with us.

In the specific verse quoted above, Jesus is referring to worry over what we wear. This reference to clothing represents our concerns about all of our material needs, for his answer to all of those worries is the same: God will provide. King Solomon was known for his grand robes and the beauty of his palace, as well as his wisdom. Jesus could not have chosen a better standard against which to measure the beauty of nature, and no doubt all of his listeners got the point. If God does a better job creating beauty in exquisite flowers than Solomon's tailors were able to do with his robes, how much more is God able to do for us? Indeed, God's efforts always far exceed ours—so why worry? One would worry only if one failed to trust God and did not really believe in the depth and breadth and height of God's love for humankind.

These words of Jesus are not offered in a glib way that overlooks the seriousness of the need for material goods. Rather they point to an altered sense of priorities and an altered placement of trust—from this world to God. Although it may be reasonable to talk with your church finance committee frankly about your financial needs from time to time, or even to consult with your denominational official if you are simply not able to live on the wage paid you, there is a difference between being responsible about one's legitimate needs and being consumed with worry about them or simply being greedy and wanting more. Trust in God—you will have what you need now and always.

The second complaint I have heard over the years is "I don't have enough time." This is a valid concern for well intentioned people who want very much to spread the love of God in Christ to all they meet. There is always one more visit to make, one more letter to write, one more sermon point to make, and one more prayer to offer.

The seductive part of this desire to do more and more, however, is the subtle message that without me the Kingdom cannot come. This particular complaint is one that I am uniquely qualified to speak about since it is an issue that I have faced many times in my life.

I was forced to recognize the depths of my illusion about my own powers when confronted with my own mortality. Seven years ago I was diagnosed with breast cancer and faced the greatest physical and spiritual challenge that I have ever had. As I sat listening to the doctor read the lab results of the biopsy he had taken a few days earlier, I was transformed from being a capable person able to think and reason and make decisions into a child who lacked confidence and the analytical ability to decide anything, much less which life-saving surgery I should choose.

Over the next nine months of repeated hospitalizations, surgeries, and chemotherapy treatments, I had a great deal of time to examine my life and priorities. As difficult as that time period and the year following it were, I would not trade them for anything were I given the chance. As grueling and frightening as they were, they were also rich times of blessing for me and my family, as we were surrounded by the community of faith and graced with God's presence in wonderfully healing ways. I learned much about myself and about my God during that time.

I learned, for example, that I was more spiritually arrogant than I would have ever imagined possible. Having been raised to believe in myself and to think I could do whatever I put my mind to, I had drifted across the line of healthy self-esteem into a life that had as its premise my self-sufficiency and (unexamined) omnipotence. I saw during that extended time of reflection that on some level I really did believe that the Kingdom depended upon me and my efforts—I was not a cog in a wheel; I was the Wheel!

After months of forced inactivity and being waited on by countless friends and neighbors and also by my husband and children, I began to see that heretofore I had been quite good at giving help but not so good at receiving it. I did not consciously think I was better than others or consciously believe that I did not need anyone else. My arrogance was far more subtle, and it was only in the face of my great need for others to perform the daily tasks that I was used to doing on top of working full time—shopping, food preparation and clean-up, laundry, picking up children at school—that I discovered it. I saw that I really had believed that I was all-powerful and invincible. With cancer came the spiritual breakthrough that enabled me to see the lie in that belief. I was not self-sufficient and all-powerful—I was like everybody else: at times able and at other times unable to function on my own.

I remember the night when I was thinking about these new revelations about myself. As I lay on the couch I felt something move inside me. There was no audible sound or physical sensation accompanying the realization. It was at a much deeper level—in my soul itself. An enormous weight was lifted from my shoulders; I remember saying, "Oh, I don't have to do it all. You can instead." I felt ever so much lighter and lighthearted. For the first time in as long as I could remember I felt free to simply be a cog in the wheel—how liberating and invigorating!

Along with this new sense of freedom I found that my use of time could be different as well. Since I no longer had to do it all, I could take time to enjoy life as I went along. I began to allow myself to read books I had always wanted to read, to watch an occasional television show, to play more often with my children and my dog, to spend more time with my husband.

My prayer life changed as well. I noticed that I spent more time listening to God and less time talking. I began to understand at a much deeper level than ever before what it means to say "Thy will be done" in my life. And I began to be more dependent upon God in my daily walk in all areas of my life.

Perhaps you have known similar struggles with time and how you use it. A scripture that speaks to the problem at the heart of the matter—namely, reliance upon self instead of upon God—is found in Paul's first letter to the church at Corinth. Addressing what must have been factions in the church, which threatened the unity of the household of faith, Paul wrote: "I planted, Apollos watered, but God gave the growth" (1 Corinthians 3:6).

Apollos was a Jew from Alexandria who played a prominent part in the early church (Acts 18:24). When he traveled to Corinth his eloquence as a speaker led to a group springing up in the community of faith that claimed him as a mentor. Paul understood the threat to the community of relying on human wisdom (1 Corinthians 1:18–2:10) and went out of his way to stress the commonality of purpose between himself and Apollos. In the simple verse quoted above he spoke truths that echo down the ages and that need to be heard by every pastor.

In these nine words Paul speaks about the unequal partnership between God and humanity. To be sure, both he and Apollos had their roles in the work of the church; God had called both of them and given them unique and important gifts to be used for the furtherance of the realm of God here on earth. Paul reminded the people at Corinth that he and Apollos were unified in their goals and important in their contributions. They were not, however, the ones that made it all work.

When it was asked who was responsible for the changes in the lives of the believers, the only answer was God. It was God who had shown the great light in the midst of the darkness, which Isaiah spoke of, by sending Jesus Christ into the world so that all might be saved. It was God who had rescued God's people from lives of desperation and meaninglessness and instead offered lives of joy and reconciliation and love. It was God who had done all of these things—not Paul or Apollos. They were important cogs in the wheel who were faithful to their calling; but they were not the Wheel themselves.

This lesson is an important one for those of us who would like to be ordained leaders. It has profound implications for our lives in every area, especially our use of time. When I failed to remember that God alone enables growth and change in our lives, I became more dependent upon myself and turned away from God ever so slightly. In so doing, I shut myself off from the source of my strength and wisdom and love ever so slightly as well. Although I did not know it, I was less resourceful and creative because I was relying primarily on myself and my own capacity to reason. The ministry I offered, I am now convinced, was stunted because of it.

In contrast, when I realized with Paul that *God* and God alone gives the growth, then I became more dependent on God and less dependent on myself in responsible ways. At the same time, I experienced a liberation from former ways of thinking in many spheres and found that my creativity was increasing by leaps and bounds. I had discovered the benefits of tapping into the Creator! These may seem like strange things for a person who had already been ordained for fifteen years prior to this discovery to be saying; nevertheless, they are true.

I offer one more set of categories that may help you as you move into seminary and then into ministry. Although they are categories about different ways of understanding time, they can help you as you consider issues of money and leadership and worship and crisis and any other things that come your way in ministry. They are the two Greek words *kairos* and *chronos.*

Chronos refers to measurable time by which we mark our lives—minutes, days, weeks, years. It is clock or calendar time, which is quantitative, measurable, and repetitive. When we think only in terms of *chronos* we see the sands in the hourglass running out and are aware of what we did not get done today. The hours of each week press on us in a burdensome way, and the stress level in our lives approaches unsafe levels. As a friend once put it, "Sunday comes quickly."

There is another way to view time, however, from the longer perspective of God's view. That view is *kairos* or "fulfilled time, the right time." *Kairos* points to unique temporal moments that are filled with special meaning. It appears frequently in the New *pregnant moments* Testament and refers specifically to the unique advent of Christ, who came "in the fullness of time." Throughout history, Christians have interpreted events in which their experience and knowledge of God is especially keen as *kairos* times that bring them closer to the Deity.

There will be (and probably already have been) times in your life that you will describe in terms of *kairos*. These will be times in which you feel God's presence more keenly, get a clearer view of a situation as it relates to God's will, and look back and see the hand of God in the way the events unfolded—all with greater clarity and sense of relatedness to God's purpose.

The night I at last laid down the burden of being omnipotent was such a *kairos* time. It remains etched in my memory as an occasion of God's grace that left me forever changed. You will have such times, too, in ministry when the way is clearer, the struggle abates, hope is restored, the path made straight. In those moments you will know that however much *chronos* time affects our daily lives from moment to moment, it is in *kairos* that we really live and move and have our being; it is in *kairos* that we meet God and are changed for the better.

Do not allow yourself while in seminary to be hounded by the demands of a world living only by the *chronos* of the clock. Remember that there is another kind of time, and cultivate your awareness of it by turning to God each day. When you do experience God's *kairos*, you will be freed for a time from the frustrated feeling that you can never finish it all, for you will know that you were never called to do so in the first place. You will be content to let God be God and yourself to be the creature, not the Creator. Such a perspective will enable you to be about the work of ministry while maintaining a sense of balance and equilibrium in your life and work.

EXERCISE

Take some time to think about issues of time and money. Ask yourself the following questions: How do I feel about money? Do I want to have a lot of it? What does having money mean to me? What lessons did I learn about its value as I was growing up? How do I feel about having less money than my parishioners or friends?

Think about your money management and stewardship. Do you have a budget and stick to it? Are you able to save for emergencies, plan for your future, make financial contributions to church? If not what can you do to make changes in your money management? If you are married, do your financial dreams match those of your spouse?

Thinking now about time and how you use it, make a list of your weekly obligations and the time spent at each one. Calculate how many hours are accounted for out of the 168 allotted to you each week. How many hours are left? Do you feel you are living a reasonable schedule, or do you feel stressed and tired and irritable all or some of the time? If you answered yes to the latter question, how can you make some changes in the way you manage your time?

Think about the scripture passages of this chapter. How do Jesus' words about the lilies and Paul's words about God's giving the growth affect you?

Finally, what changes do you want to make in your life now as a result of these reflections. You might want to discuss them with a trusted family member, friend, or fellow student. Consider sharing with that person your plan for change and asking for prayer as you endeavor to live a different way. Your sharing will help that person to hold you lovingly accountable for the changes you say you want to make.

Prayer: Most gracious and loving God, out of the past and out of your love you have created me in unique and wonderful ways. You have given me the gift of life and spread out before me all of the days of that life. Enable me to live each one of them in the certain knowledge that they are filled already with your all-sufficient grace and that I have only to walk closely with you and all of the things I need will be added to me. Quiet my restless heart, free me from all worry and concern, speak to me in the stillness of the moment, enable me to live fully and confidently every day of my life. In Christ's name I pray. Amen.

CHAPTER 8

The Seminary Experience: An Overview

See, I am making all things new. Revelation 21:5

I fear no evil for you are with me. Psalm 23:4

The best thing is that I sit on your lap and you scratch my back . . . that and the cookies! Mitchell Cetuk

 while ago I was talking with my son Mitchell about church and asking him what he thought about it. He characteristically dismissed his hours in church as a waste of perfectly good time in which he could be doing something really valuable, like playing with his friends. He then paused and was silent for a moment. I asked him what he was thinking about and he replied: "The best thing is that I sit on your lap and you scratch my back . . . that and the cookies!"

The thing that mattered most to Mitchell was the feeling of warmth and love he felt sitting on my lap during the long church service, that and the cookies after the service. He did not care what was being said or preached about, he did not care about what was being sung, he did not even care what the pastor did during the children's sermon. The value of church for Mitchell was not in the message, it was in the relationships (and the food!). It was here that he met God and felt loved by God.

There is a sense in which Mitchell's priorities match what is primary in the seminary experience, namely, the developing relationships through which you come to know God more fully. If you allow yourself to be open to the total experience, your relationships with yourself, with others, and with God will be enriched and changed. You will come to know yourself more intimately than ever before through conversations and study and worship. You will gain knowledge about what it means to be human and how people live their lives on a daily basis while pursuing their

dreams. In the classroom and community you will forge friendships that are deep and lasting and in which the things that are
most important to you in life are shared. Through this process you
will come to know God better as well.

One way to describe the evolutionary process that most seminarians go through is to name it "formation." In an earlier chapter
I discussed the formation process of psychiatric residents. Without
repeating that material in detail, I want to remind you of the
dynamics of any formation process.

Simply put, formation requires a person to die to the self; to give
up former ways of being and thinking and believing and relating;
to renegotiate one's belief systems about oneself and the world;
and to replace old ways of being with new, more sophisticated and
lasting ways of being that are more appropriate to the new role in
society that one is preparing to take.

My husband has been in law enforcement for the past twenty-
five years. During that time he has had the opportunity to work
with young rookie cops, who are just starting out in their careers,
as well as more seasoned officers, who long ago stopped thinking
of themselves as civilians. In his current assignment at the police
academy, he teaches new recruits and develops continuing education for seasoned officers. I have learned a lot from Norm about the
process of formation that is peculiar to police recruits in some
ways but can also be generalized to other vocations.

The challenge facing police recruits is great: they must go from
living comfortably in a civilian world to living comfortably within
a highly militarized system with a definite chain of command that
must be respected and worked within at all times. They must go
from thinking in the individualized fashion typical of Western
thought to thinking as part of a team and caring as much for their
partner's safety as their own.

I recall one time when my husband came home at the end of the
day amused by something that had happened with the recruits.
Assigned lockers at the beginning of the program, they were
required to have their gear stowed in a particular fashion and the
combination locks set properly as they left the locker room. An
inspection by one of the drill sergeants revealed a combination
lock that was not secure. As a result the gear of the two recruits

sharing the locker was removed and piled up on the gym floor. The two recruits were given a very short time in which to retrieve their own gear and take it to their lockers where it would, at last, be properly secured. For the following week the entire class was prohibited from using their lockers overnight. That meant that at the end of each day they had to remove all the things in their lockers and take them home. At the start of the next day they would have to reverse the process. This was no small assignment since each recruit receives several items necessary for police training. Clearly this discipline was a hardship for the entire class. Because of the sloppiness of one person, all people paid the price.

When I heard the story, I wondered what the lesson was for all of the recruits and asked Norm what was to be gained. His response was that the recruits needed to learn to pay strict attention to detail, for someone's life might depend upon it. What if a police officer did not properly secure weapons in a police station? What would stop someone being arrested from stealing a weapon and turning it upon everyone in the station? Further, they needed to know that their actions (however unimportant they may seem) could have dire consequences for their fellow officers. In other words, they needed to begin to live out of a collective consciousness and stop thinking only about themselves.

This example from quite a different walk of life highlights what is meant by "formation process." The recruits had to change the way they were thinking and behaving; they had to begin to think like police officers and to act accordingly. The entire program, grueling as it was, was designed to weed out the people who were not cut out for the lifestyle that goes with being a police officer. It was also designed to simulate the challenges facing police and the mind-set required to succeed and be safe. There was a time when I thought the program was unnecessarily harsh. I have come to see that it must be that way—so difficult is it for recruits to give up former ways of being that would be downright dangerous in the line of duty.

The same degree of difficulty is sometimes present for seminarians. Although you are not faced with learning to live in a military system, you are, nonetheless, faced with the prospect of changing from a layperson into a clergyperson. Clergy need to be able to offer leadership in an increasingly complex and secularized society; need to have a strong and vibrant faith; need to have courage to meet and challenge the principalities and powers of society; and need to have a wellspring of love for people of all ages, races, temperaments, maturity levels, and economic levels.

The hard work of seminary sometimes serves to weed out people who belong elsewhere. It is also designed to help you learn to think critically, as a ministerial leader must think; to become aware of your gifts and your limitations; and to open your eyes to the human condition in its complexity and beauty. You need to begin to think like a clergyperson thinks and to see God at work everywhere and in everyone.

The crucible of the seminary experience offers an unparalleled opportunity for spiritual growth. Anyone who wants to be ordained must be spiritually mature. That means that if you are seeking ordination, then the following description must fit who you are. Read the next paragraph carefully and ask yourself whether it is descriptive of you at this point in time.

Reliance upon God must be first nature for any good pastoral leader. Patience in the face of slow-moving change must come easily. Courage to speak the truth in love must be readily available. Ability to think clearly and chart a course into the future for oneself and one's people that is guided by the gospel of Jesus Christ is critical. Do these attributes describe you at this point in time?

One of the ways I think about theological education and the seminary experience is to view it as an extended crisis in the lives of the students. If you have been in seminary for a while, you know that you are being challenged on every level of your being: physically, emotionally, and spiritually. You are being pushed to examine what you once thought were secure beliefs and are perhaps wondering what they will be replaced with, if anything.

Although crises of this magnitude may not always be comfortable, they hold within them the seeds of new life and rebirth. As the caterpillar turns into a beautiful butterfly after a period of hard work in the cocoon, the crisis of seminary can result in a new and beautiful creation as well, namely, YOU!

I have discussed throughout this book the key that can make the difference between a time of joy and challenge and excitement (albeit at times difficult) and an endlessly negative and discouraging three (or more) years. That difference is your mind-set.

As I looked at the many different aspects of seminary life—classroom, community life, exploration of the call to ministry, supervised ministry, time and money management—I pointed out the choices you have in the way you view them. In every case you have the same choice, namely, to view each aspect in a negative way or to reframe it and see it as the opportunity it is for spiritual growth. In every case I have cited scripture that speaks to the issue and offered examples of how you might gain spiritual maturity through the particular challenge under discussion. At the end of each chapter I have included an exercise for you to do with a colleague that will help you put to use the reflections in each chapter. I have concluded each section appropriately with prayer. If you adopt the methodology I have used, you will be well on your way in the formation process because you will be relying more and more upon God and God's word for your response to the circumstances in your life.

I offer two final passages from scripture that summarize for me the process of theological education. They come from Hebrew and from Christian scriptures and are beloved in the community of faith: Psalm 23:4 and Revelation 21:5.

In John's magnificent vision of the revelation of the consummation of history, we read about the second coming of Christ and the end of time as we know it. In chapter 21, John records his vision of the new heaven and the new earth and the new Jerusalem. Early in the chapter he records God saying, "See, I am making all things new."

This passage echoes through the years and confirms my experience of God, for when I encounter the living God through Christ, I come away from the encounter changed for the better in some important way. I am usually calmer, more centered, better focused, and more certain of how to proceed. If I have come to God in fear, I come away from God at peace. If I am troubled by circumstances in my life, I gain a perspective on those troubles that calms me and helps me to relax and be more confident that all will be well. If I am confused about the direction I should take, I find the path made more clear when I listen for God's direction. Over the years, I have found that the cumulative effect of my prayer time has been that I have become more disciplined, more courageous, more confident, and more joyous. There is no question in my mind that I have been made new over and over again through my relationship with the living God.

If you walk closely with God through your time in seminary, you will likewise be changed for the better. I cannot predict what these changes will be; I can only predict that you will be changed for the better, for God works through theological education to mold and shape us and fit us for work in the vineyard. The opportunity for you to be so shaped is before you; you have only to embrace it.

The second scripture I offer you now is found in the most frequently read scripture of all time. The Twenty-third Psalm is David's beautiful description of the intimate love of God for the creation. It graphically portrays the many ways that the shepherd anticipates the needs of the sheep and is tireless in meeting those needs for protection, sustenance, and healing.

The shepherd knows that sheep are not very intelligent animals; they are easily spooked, do not know how to protect themselves and wander easily from the safety of the flock. Robbers love to steal them, other animals love to eat them, and the natural elements (like running water) can prove deadly to them.

David knew all of this when he wrote Psalm 23. The entire psalm speaks of the great love of the shepherd for the sheep. Verse 4 is written from the sheep's perspective. "Even though I walk through the darkest valley, I fear no evil; for you are with me." Because the sheep know that the shepherd is totally focused on their well-being, even evil itself is not frightening. The sheep proceed through the narrow pass unafraid because there is no reason to fear, even though there may be thieves and robbers waiting in the pass.

The same can be said of seminary. If you cultivate your relationship with and reliance upon God through your experience in the classroom and community, you will know more and more how trustworthy and reliable God is. You will learn that the exact opposite of fear *is* love, as John tells us (1 John 4:18), and that when you are in God's presence all fears and apprehensions will vanish. You will grow in courage, in power, and in grace and will be increasingly able to handle the sometimes enormous pressures of seminary life.

I hope that while in seminary you will make a habit of attending chapel services if they are held weekly. At Drew, the chapel is the centerpiece of our community life. We come together three days a week to sing and praise God, to share in prayer, and to receive the sacrament of Holy Communion. These sacred times of worship draw us together, remind us why we have come, and give us strength to continue on the journey.

Sometimes chapel attendance drops as the semester wears on. At those times I gently remind the community that in times of stress and great need we must draw closer to God through worship instead of drifting away. I remind you of the same. Try to find ways to maintain your practice of the spiritual disciplines during the semester. Remember that reading scripture for an exegesis paper is different from reading it for spiritual sustenance. Make attending chapel services a priority during your week, and encourage others to do the same. These things are crucial to your formation as a pastoral-spiritual leader, as well as to your sanity.

I come to the end of this book somewhat reluctant to stop. I would like to throw you a lifeline to enable you to hang on and flourish while in seminary. In effect, I have already thrown the line out to you. Will you take it? I hope and pray that you will. You may not understand all of what is being said during your time at seminary; you may have doubts and fears, questions and concerns. All of that is appropriate for this time in your life. I hope, however, that quick on the heels of any doubts or fears you may have is the certain knowledge that you are not alone and that God has not called you into this journey of faith development to leave you stranded and confused. Rather, God is with you always, even "to the end of the age. . . . " If you know that, then you can say with David that, though you walk through the valley, you will fear nothing, not even evil, for you know God walks with you. Hence, you already have all you will ever really need.

EXERCISE

Take some time to review the issues discussed in this book by glancing through the table of contents. What are your current thoughts about each topic now? You might want to review the exercises in each chapter and ask yourself whether your answers to the questions posed are different now than they once were.

Meditate upon God's declaration in Revelation 21:5, "See, I am making all things new!" In what ways are you a new creature? How have you changed since coming to seminary? In what ways would you like to change?

Think about how God is working in your life to bring about the formation needed to prepare you for a life of service in ministry. To what extent do you count on and cultivate God's presence in your life? Are you resisting God's direction or welcoming it? Have you maintained your practice of the spiritual disciplines while in seminary? How is this practice (or lack of it) affecting your life and work in seminary?

Close by meditating on Psalm 23. Close your eyes, relax, and say the words slowly, verse by verse. Allow the images to come alive for you in your mind's eye, and see yourself walking with the Good Shepherd. Talk with the Good Shepherd when you have finished repeating the psalm and share your joys and sorrows, your dreams and frustrations. Remember the great love of the Shepherd for the sheep and be joyful and at peace.

Prayer: Most Gracious God, I am grateful for your loving presence in my life and in the community of faith. Create me anew in your image, lead me to the still waters, restore my soul. Strengthen me for the life of service to which you have called me and make me fit to work in your vineyard. Help me to be faithful to your claim upon my life in all I say and do, and grant that I may be a faithful witness to you and an effective channel for your grace. In Christ's name I pray. Amen.

NOTES

1. THE TASKS OF MINISTRY

1. My mother's enthusiasm was tempered by her knowledge of society in the early 1960s, which still clearly dictated acceptable roles for men and women. At that time ordained ministry was not an acceptable position for women although the Methodist Church had been ordaining women since 1950. There were not many women ordained at the time of my call; in fact, when I was ordained deacon in 1974 I was the first clergywoman I had ever met!

2. Seward Hiltner, *Preface to Pastoral Theology* (Nashville: Abingdon, 1958), 69.

3. Ibid., 181.

4. Ibid., 201.

5. For this conceptual framework for understanding the work of the ordained pastoral leader I am indebted to Dr. Randall Nichols, Director of the Doctor of Ministry Program at Princeton Theological Seminary, Princeton, New Jersey.

6. C. S. Lewis coined this title for God after the death of his beloved wife, whom he met and married late in life. It is perhaps the most searing description I have ever heard for the God whom many believe to be the source of untimely and, hence, unfair death. See his book *A Grief Observed* for a complete discussion of his grief and his theological struggles over his wife's death. Although it is a difficult book to read, it should be required reading for every pastor.

7. In Paul's Second Letter to the Corinthians he wrote about the things he had suffered since his conversion. Beatings, stonings, shipwrecks, hunger, thirst, nakedness, and imprisonment were his lot as an ambassador for Christ. Rather than make him bitter, however, these things served to make him more reliant upon God through Christ. While others might have turned against God, Paul understood that through these trials and his weaknesses he could revel in God's strength. He had discovered that when he was weak, then he was strong in Christ (2 Corinthians 11:24–12:10).

8. Frederick Buechner, *Wishful Thinking: A Theological ABC* (New York: Harper & Row, 1973), 95.

9. Maya Angelou, *Wouldn't Take Nothing for My Journey Now* (New York: Bantam Books, 1994), 15.

2. WRESTLING WITH HOLY THINGS

1. "The Order for the Administration of the Sacrament of Baptism," in *The Methodist Hymnal* (Nashville: The Methodist Publishing House, 1966), 828.

2. Janet Fishburn's work in progress about the current state of theological education notes that all of the Protestant theological schools she studied in depth during a recent sabbatical were in some stage of noticing and lamenting the lack of attention paid by the faculty and structure of the curriculum to students' spiritual formation. While all schools studied were striving to address these important issues, all were also somewhat at a loss about how to do so adequately.

3. Sharon Parks, *The Critical Years* (San Francisco: Harper, 1986), 134-35.

4. H. Richard Niebuhr, *The Purpose of the Church and Its Ministry* (New York: Harper & Brothers, 1956), 118. The reader is invited to consider Niebuhr's insights alongside those of the Brazilian educator Paulo Freire in his work *Pedagogy of the Oppressed* (New York: Continuum, 1970). Freire critiques the pedagogy that assumes a hierarchical model of learning comprised of but one teacher and many learners in a classroom. Niebuhr's classic text, written fourteen years before Freire's critique of Western pedagogy in general, raises the same concerns about the arrogance implicit in that model. Niebuhr argues (as does Freire after him) that in such an atmosphere, "intellectual activity is at a minimum in both parties; such a school is not a community of students but a propaganda or indoctrination institution" (117).

5. Evelyn Underhill, *The Spiritual Life* (Harrisburg: Morehouse Publishing, 1955), 43.

6. When I use the phrase "gentle narcissistic arrogance," I am, of course, commenting on the natural proclivity most of us have to assume the correctness of our own views. I am not speaking of the arrogance associated with more blatant and overt disregard for others or a pathological inability to consider another's view or feelings found in, for example, the sociopath.

7. Paul Watzlawick, *The Language of Change: Elements of Therapeutic Communication* (New York: Basic Books, 1978), 119.

8. Paul Watzlawick, John H. Weakland, and Richard Fisch, *Change: Principles of Problem Formation and Problem Resolution* (New York: W. W. Norton, 1974), 95.

9. A contemporary translation of "Abba" is the affectionate and familiar term "Daddy." By addressing God thus, and inviting us to do the same, Jesus was offering an intimacy with the Creator heretofore unknown. He was reframing the very core of our relationship with God by making the unknowable the familiar, and thereby collapsing the distance between the Creator and the created.

10. Dietrich Bonhoeffer, *The Cost of Discipleship*, trans. R. H. Fuller, 2d ed. (New York: Macmillan, 1963), 99. Subsequent quotes from this edition in this chapter are identified with a page number in the text.

3. THE CALL TO MINISTRY

1. *Fact Book on Theological Education for the Academic Year 1995–1996* (Pittsburgh: The Association of Theological Schools in the United States and Canada), 48.

2. Lynn Rothstein, *Consortium for Institutional Research at Theological Schools Entering Student Questionnaire 1994* (Pittsburgh: The Association of Theological Schools and the Consortium Institutions, 1994), 6.

3. *ATS Fact Book 1995–1996*, 46.

4. Ibid., 27.

5. Laypeople serving as supervisors of students in the broadest sense of the word is a widespread practice in theological education today. Called various things (Teaching Church Committee, Lay Training Committee, and so forth), the committee serves to give students both a broader source of feedback and evaluation and an arena in which to talk regularly with trusted laypeople about issues of importance in ministerial formation.

6. The *ATS Fact Book 1996–1997* notes that of 63,618 students enrolled in accredited theological schools in 1996, 41 percent (27,876) were in Master of Divinity programs, making that the degree with the highest portion of students (p. 34).

7. Philipp Melanchthon, *The Apology of the Augsburg Confession*, in *The Book of Concord: The Confessions of the Evangelical Lutheran Church*, trans. and ed. Theodore G. Tappert (Philadelphia: Muhlenberg, 1959), 269.

8. Martin Luther, "A Treatise on Christian Liberty," trans. W. A. Lambert, in *Works of Martin Luther*, vol. 2 (Philadelphia: Muhlenberg, 1943), 333.

9. Bertram Lee Woolf, *Reformation Writings of Martin Luther* (London: Lutterworth, 1952),

275, quoted in William Robinson, *Completing the Reformation: The Doctrine of the Priesthood of All Believers* (Lexington, Ky.: The College of the Bible, 1955), 11.

10. *Webster's New World Dictionary of the American Language*, College Edition (New York: The World Publishing Company, 1960), 1633.

11. Gustaf Wingren, *Luther on Vocation* (Philadelphia: Muhlenberg, 1957), 124.

12. Bertram Lee Woolf, *Reformation Writings of Martin Luther* (London: Lutterworth, 1952), 276.

13. Cyril Eastwood, *The Priesthood of All Believers: An Examination of the Doctrine from the Reformation to the Present Day* (London: The Epworth Press, 1960), 60.

14. Martin Luther, "The Babylonian Captivity of the Church," trans. A. T. W. Steinhaeuser, in *Works of Martin Luther*, vol. 2 (Philadelphia: Muhlenberg, 1943), 279.

15. Presbyterian Church (USA), *Book of Order* (Louisville: Office of the General Assembly, 1994), G-6.0101-102, G-6.0105.

16. *The Book of Discipline of The United Methodist Church* (Nashville: The United Methodist Publishing House, 1996), 301.

17. *Candidacy Manual for the Evangelical Lutheran Church in America* (Chicago: Division for Ministry, 1995), 11.

18. Denominations vary in the length of time one must be a church member before beginning the ordination process. The Evangelical Lutheran Church in America, the United Church of Christ, and The United Methodist Church all require a minimum of one year membership. The Presbyterian Church (USA) requires a six-month minimum membership prior to beginning the process. All denominations assume active participation in the life of the congregation. In these churches, along with the Episcopal Church and the churches comprising the Baptist tradition, the local congregation must give assent and support to the candidacy of a particular person. If such support is not given, the person seeking ordination will not be permitted to continue in the process.

In addition, denominations vary on the degree to which they are involved in a student's enrolling in seminary. United Methodist candidates apply to seminary independently of any movement through the ordination process. In the Evangelical Lutheran Church, however, students require the support of the Candidacy Committee before beginning their theological studies (*Candidacy Manual*, 8).

19. Presbyterian Church (USA), *Book of Order*, G-14.0302, G-14.0304.

20. "Entrance Procedures into Licensed and Ordained Ministry," in *The Book of Discipline of The United Methodist Church* (Nashville: The United Methodist Publishing House, 1996), 305.

21. Ibid., 304.

22. Evangelical Lutheran Church in America, *Candidacy Manual*, 12.

4. LIFE TOGETHER: VARIETY AND COMMUNITY

1. Students who have been forced out of former occupations are, I believe, particularly vulnerable and need to do some serious reflection about the reasons they are in seminary. Support found in church at this difficult time of transition, with its attending dynamics of shame and despair and fear, can be confused with a call to ministry. If you had no real choice but to leave your former work situation, be sure to explore the degree to which your decision to come to seminary is linked to that painful reality. It is a wonderful thing to find support in the church in our hour of need; it is another thing entirely to enter seminary feeling called to ministry because of that support.

2. For a complete discussion of Erikson's stages, see Erik Erikson's *Childhood and Society*, 2d rev. ed. (New York: W. W. Norton, 1963), chap. 7; and *Identity and the Life Cycle* (New York: International Universities Press, 1959), chap. 2.

3. *Fact Book on Theological Education for the Academic Year 1996–1997* (Pittsburgh: The Association of Theological Schools in the United States and Canada), 38-39.

4. As larger segments of the population are living longer, we are seeing greater numbers of students in seminary who bear major responsibility for the care of elderly parents. This is true of both single and married students. The phenomenon can both sensitize the community and the curriculum to issues of health care and medical ethics and necessitate greater numbers of students taking part-time course loads or leaves of absence.

5. *ATS Fact Book 1996–1997*, 38-39.

6. David Augsburger, *Conflict Mediation Across Cultures: Pathways and Patterns* (Louisville: Westminster/John Knox, 1992), 22.

7. *ATS Fact Book 1996–1997*, 66-67.

8. *Webster's New World Dictionary of the American Language* (New York: The World Publishing Company, 1960), 354. The three meanings listed are: "(1) a container made of graphite, porcelain, platinum, or other substance that can resist great heat, for meting and calcining ores, metals, etc.; (2) the hollow at the bottom of an ore furnace, where the molten metal collects; (3) a severe test; hard trial."

9. For a more complete discussion of the Tower and its place within the history of Israel, see Bernhard W. Anderson, *Understanding the Old Testament* (Englewood Cliffs, N.J.: Prentice-Hall, 1957), 160-87.

5. THE CLASSROOM

1. H. Richard Niebuhr, *The Purpose of the Church and Its Ministry* (New York: Harper and Bros., 1956), 118.

2. Psalm 139:14.

3. Robert Coles, *The Spiritual Life of Children* (Boston: Houghton Mifflin, 1990), 108.

4. This was before the 1968 merger between The Methodist Church and The Evangelical United Brethren Church, which formed The United Methodist Church.

5. See Milton Rokeach, *The Open and Closed Mind* (New York: Basic Books, 1960), for a more complete and quite interesting discussion of his findings. Those interested in vocations that will place them in leadership positions in which they attempt to move others from point A to point B would do well to familiarize themselves with Rokeach's work. His insights provide helpful categories with which to analyze responses to new ideas and programs.

6. Ibid., 286.

7. Ibid., 62-63, 186.

8. Rokeach found that people with closed minds consistently had greater difficulty in synthesizing and integrating new beliefs and, thereby, creating a new system of beliefs. He also found that they evidenced a greater anxiety in the face of new learning and that they were more frequently defensive in response. Their defensive posture contributed to their inability to absorb new information; in other words, they did not learn as much as did their open-minded colleagues.

9. Ibid., 361.

10. See Edward Leroy Long Jr., *Higher Education as a Moral Enterprise* (Washington, D.C.: Georgetown University Press, 1992), chapter 2, for an interesting discussion about the nature of education and the ways it has evolved in this country.

11. While Professor Long is writing in particular about the enterprise of higher education, I find his arguments entirely appropriate to elementary and secondary education as well. Indeed, if we do not teach our children when they are in elementary school how to be mindful of themselves and the social context in which they live, along with assisting them to master information they will need to be independent and responsible adults, then we have failed them. Such gaps in their education will, I believe, be extremely difficult (if not impossible) to fill in higher education.

12. Leonard I. Sweet, widely known as a leader and prophet of the church today, refers to the church of tomorrow as the "Ancient/Future" Church. The term captures the roots of the

church in the past as well as the recognition that the church can and must change in response to shifts in the wider culture in which it is situated.

13. Joseph C. Hough Jr. and John B. Cobb Jr., *Christian Identity and Theological Education* (Chico, Calif.: Scholars Press, 1985), 115.

14. Miroslav Volf, "Teachers, Crusts and Toppings," *The Christian Century* (7-14 February 1996): 133.

15. William G. Perry Jr., *Forms of Intellectual and Ethical Development in the College Years* (New York: Holt, Rinehart and Winston, 1968), 16-27.

16. Required course in the area of Church and Society.

17. John Wesley, "At the Opening of a School in Kingswood," in *Hymns for Children* (1763), 35-36, reprinted in *The Works of John Wesley*, vol. 7, ed. Franz Hildebrandt and Oliver A. Beckerlegge (Nashville: Abingdon, 1989), 644.

18. Psalm 121 is called "The Traveler's Psalm" and is a beautiful song about God's abiding presence with us wherever we go. It is a particularly good one for seminarians who are journeying deep into themselves in order to then journey out into the world as leaders with spiritual depth and integrity. If you are not already familiar with it, I suggest that you read it often. If you do you will be lifted up and encouraged by it.

6. THE PRACTICE OF MINISTRY

1. Donald Light, *Becoming Psychiatrists: The Professional Transformation of Self* (New York: W. W. Norton, 1980), 244.

2. For a complete discussion of these elements of moral transition, see Light, "The Moral Career of the Psychiatric Resident," chap. 11 in *Becoming Psychiatrists.*

7. MONEY AND TIME MANAGEMENT

1. *The Book of Discipline of The United Methodist Church* (Nashville: The United Methodist Publishing House, 1996), ¶ 321.4*d*.

2. Data taken from the *Fact Book on Theological Education for the Academic Year 1996–1997* (Pittsburgh: The Association of Theological Schools in the United States and Canada, 1997), 98.

3. Ibid., 97.

4. Anthony Ruger and Barbara G. Wheeler, *Manna from Heaven? Theological and Rabbinical Student Debt,* Auburn Studies, no. 2 (New York: Auburn Theological Seminary, 1995), 6.

5. Anthony Ruger, *An Analysis of Educational Debt Among Theological and Rabbinical Students,* Auburn Center Background Report Series, no. 5 (New York: Auburn Theological Seminary, November 1995), figure 4.2.3.

6. The general rule is that for every hour in class you will need to spend two hours studying outside of class.

7. I am assuming here that you will take one hour per meal, three times a day, seven days a week.

8. This student commutes one hour each way and makes four trips to campus each week.

9. Pastor Adams spends between 30 and 45 minutes throughout the day in personal devotional time. It is the foundation of everything Pastor Adams does the rest of the day.

10. This assumes that for every minute in the sermon there is one hour of preparation.

11. Pastor Adams meets weekly with the local clergy association, is active with the senior citizens organization, and is on the Board of Directors of the County Homeless Shelter/Food Bank.

12. Pastor Adams is active at the denominational level approximately four hours per month.

13. Pastor Adams attends church suppers, helps at rummage sales, helps prepare meals for homeless guests in the church, works at the Youth Group's car wash, and so on. These events do not occur every week, hence I am suggesting three hours per week on average.

14. This schedule shows two hours of family time per day on average. Some days, however, Pastor Adams spends no time with the family beyond mealtimes.